Fort Marion Prisoners
and the Trauma of
Native Education

The Catch, Bear's Heart, Ledger Book Drawing.
National Museum of the American Indian, Smithsonian
Institution (D206231).

Fort Marion Prisoners and the Trauma of Native Education

DIANE GLANCY

University of Nebraska Press

Lincoln and London

Library of Congress Cataloging-in-Publication Data
Glancy, Diane.
Fort Marion prisoners and the trauma of native education / Diane Glancy.
pages   cm
Summary: "Narratives of Kiowa, Cheyenne, Arapaho, Comanche
and Caddo prisoners taken to Ft. Marion, Florida, in 1875
interspersed with the author's own history and contemporary
reflections of place and identity"—Provided by publisher.
Includes bibliographical references.
ISBN 978-0-8032-4967-7 (paperback: alk. paper)
ISBN 978-0-8032-5694-1 (epub)
ISBN 978-0-8032-5695-8 (mobi)
ISBN 978-0-8032-5693-4 (pdf)
1. Indians of North America—Relocation—Florida—Castillo
de San Marcos National Monument (Saint Augustine) 2. Indian
prisoners—Florida—Castillo de San Marcos National Monument
(Saint Augustine) 3. Prisoners of war—Florida—Castillo de
San Marcos National Monument (Saint Augustine) 4. Indians,
Treatment of—Florida—Castillo de San Marcos National
Monument (Saint Augustine) 5. Indians of North America—Ethnic
identity. 6. Cherokee Indians—Biography. 7. Castillo de San Marcos
National Monument (Saint Augustine, Fla.)—History. I. Title.
E98.R4G53 2014   975.9'18—dc23   2014012342

Set in Adobe Caslon Pro by Renni Johnson.
Designed by Rachel Gould.

They are beginning to read and write. They have learned the Lord's prayer. . . . Here were men who had committed murder upon helpless women and children sitting like docile children at the feet of women learning to read. . . . It was my privilege to preach to them every Sunday, and upon week days I told them stories from the Bible . . .

BISHOP H. B. WHIPPLE
to the *New York Daily Tribune*, March 24, 1876

From Richard Henry Pratt, *Battlefield and Classroom: Four Decades with the American Indian, 1876–1904*

CONTENTS

Fort Marion Prisoners
and the Trauma of
Native Education

Fort Marion Prisoners

1875–1878

In 1875 at the end of the Southern Plains Indian Wars, seventy-two of the worst prisoners were taken by train from Fort Sill in Indian Territory, which later became Oklahoma, to an abandoned stone fort on the Atlantic Ocean: Fort Marion in St. Augustine, Florida.

The Indians had been defeated by the U.S. Cavalry. The buffalo had been slaughtered. A way of life was gone. After a council in the Wichita Mountains near Fort Sill, the Indians rode with a white flag to surrender.

From Fort Sill the prisoners rode shackled in wagons to Caddo, Indian Territory, some 165 miles east. Then they went by train to Sedalia, Missouri, Kansas City, and Fort Leavenworth, Kansas. After two weeks at Fort Leavenworth they traveled across Missouri to the St. Charles trestle bridge into St. Louis. From St. Louis, they went to Indianapolis, Louisville, Nashville, Chattanooga, Atlanta, and Macon. In Florida they stopped in Jacksonville, where the prisoners went by steamer and then railroad again for the last twenty-five miles to St. Augustine, where they made their way through crowds gathered in the street. Their journey had lasted from April 28 to May 21.

Crowds had gathered at every stop along the way. On May 19, 1875, the *Daily Louisville Commercial* reported the arrival of the train with "the hardest lot of red faces that have ever plundered and murdered Western settlers on the frontier."

But at Fort Marion, Captain Richard Henry Pratt unlocked their leg irons, cut their hair, dressed them in army uniforms, gave them ledger books in which to draw, and taught them to read and write. He also invited Clark Mills to come from Washington DC to make life casts of the captives.

The prisoners wrote letters to the U.S. government for their release, which was granted in 1878, three years after their arrival at Fort Marion. Captain Pratt's approach was one of the beginnings of a systematic effort to educate the Indians.

———————

Some of the prisoners:

> Black Horse, Comanche, his wife, Pe-ah-in,
>   and daughter, Ah-kes
> Gray Beard, Cheyenne
> Lean Bear, Cheyenne
> Ta-a-way-te, Comanche
> Making Medicine, Cheyenne
> Manimic, Cheyenne
> Howling Wolf, Cheyenne
> Bear's Heart, Cheyenne
> Toothless, Kiowa
> Wolf Stomach, Kiowa
> Sky Walker, Kiowa
> Big Nose, Cheyenne
> Dry Wood, Comanche
> White Horse, Kiowa
> Lone Wolf, Kiowa
> Spotted Elk, Cheyenne
> Heap of Birds, Cheyenne
> Wohaw, Kiowa
> Straightening an Arrow, Kiowa
> Standing Wolf, Cheyenne
> Big Moccasin, Cheyenne
> Matches, Cheyenne

Hail Stone, Cheyenne
Biter or Zo-tom, Kiowa
E-tah-dle-uh, Kiowa
White Bear, Arapaho
Hu-wah-nee, Caddo
Buffalo Meat, Cheyenne
Chief Killer, Cheyenne

All of them had several names: Making Medicine, for instance, was also called David Pendleton Oakerhater, Oakahaton, O-kuh-ha-tuh, Noksowist, Bear Going Straight, and Sun Dancer. Good Talk, a Kiowa, was also called To-keah-hi, To-un-ke-uh, To-un-keah, To-keah, Taung-ke-i-hi, Waterman, and Paul Tounkeuh.

In the morning I hear the birds before I see them. They are early risers. I put new seed in the feeder, and they shovel through it looking for sunflower seeds or what they want. Then, when the feeder is empty, they remember the seed they tossed out and hunt for it on the ground. The different tribes come for the seed—Kiowa, Cheyenne, Arapaho, Comanche, Caddo—those were the tribes.

A stereograph of a group of Indian prisoners at Fort Marion
including Black Horse and Pe-ah-in, parents of Ah-kes (front
row, middle three), labeled "Group of Comanchee Indians
in native costume confined in Fort Marion, St. Augustine,
Florida, circa 1875." O. Pierre Havens, photographer.
Photographic Study Collection, Dickinson Research Center,
National Cowboy and Western Heritage Museum,
Oklahoma City (RC2008.005.1).

Ride to Prison

After the Indians surrendered, the soldiers loaded them on wagons. It was in the darkness of midnight when soldiers chained them to the sides of the wagons.

The wife and daughter of Black Horse climbed into a wagon with him. One of the soldiers saw them. He tried to remove them from the wagon but they clung to Black Horse.

The soldiers couldn't take his wife and daughter from him—there was no one to care for them. —Didn't the soldiers have a wife and child?—Would they leave them?

The soldiers argued.

Hide between us—Black Horse told his daughter. That soldier was going to get someone. Another soldier shouted to move ahead—the wagon jumped forward—the other wagons followed. Black Horse's wife and daughter were with him—the soldier let Black Horse have them. There was *some* honor to those men.

They traveled for several days from Fort Sill to Caddo. Then they saw the box-on-wheels—They heard it scream—*EEEEEEEE*! They saw it send up smoke. It was the house-that-walks. It was the box-that-moves.

The soldiers unloaded the prisoners from the wagons and pushed them into the box. They chained the prisoners to the walls. The door slammed shut. It must have sounded like the cannon fire they remembered in battle. The house-that-walks jumped forward, moving in short jerks until the train kept moving forward and forward.

At night, the moving darkness unsettled the Indians. The noise rattled them loose from all they knew.

Most of them rode sitting in iron ropes. They were tied to the wall of the box-that-runs. The Indians had pegged their war horses to the ground—the ones they wanted to keep—the ones they didn't want taken—the ones they rode into battle.

I can't see—Ah-kes, the daughter of Black Horse cried.

Think of sitting beside me when the firelight goes out in our camp—Black Horse said. Think of the stories you heard before you fell asleep—

In the beginning, when the Maker formed people,

he put ears on the back of our head—

so we could hear what was coming from behind—

so we would not be overtaken—

but we turned our head one way then the other while he was working—

to see what he was doing—

and our ears ended up on the sides of our head.

Now we only know what happens when it is beside us—

The Train Ride

The prisoners pulled against the shackles that held them in place. They struggled in fear. They were prisoners of the Indian wars. They had been taken from their tribes. Some of the prisoners knew one another, but others had been brought to Fort Sill from other places. The prisoners only knew they were taken captive in skirmishes with the soldiers. Some of them were enemies. Gray Beard was shackled next to a warrior who had killed some of his family.

They had ridden their horses across the plains under the sky. They had followed the buffalo. The wind spoke to them. The round moon on the dew of prairie grass made a sheen that lifted the night. The sky spoke with stars. All of it was given to them from the Maker's hand. Now the land rode with the prisoners in the wagons, and in the train. When they closed their eyes, did they still see the land?

Sometimes after driving all day, the road moves before me. When I close my eyes, I still see the passing land. I think it was the same with the prisoners. They could not be separated from their *place*. If they were going, then the land was going too.

Nearly thirty years ago I worked for the State Arts Council of Oklahoma. I spent the majority of residencies at three high schools in Lawton, where the Fort Sill Military Reservation is located. After school I drove into the Wichita Mountains National Wildlife Refuge. The refuge was marked with barriers and the tracks of army vehicles where they practiced war. I climbed the 2,464-foot Mt. Scott in my car to look into the hazy distance of the surrounding prairie. Later, with the help of a friend, I took a small, red granite boulder, which I still have at my cabin in the Ozarks. I remember the sound of the Howitzers. Sometimes at school, the window panes rattled. Most of the students had lived around the world. Sometimes they didn't pay attention. They knew their parents were stationed there only for a while. The idea of transience was in the air. At the end of the week I would drive two hundred miles back to Tulsa, then return for another week.

There was a museum on the army base. It must have been where the departure of the Plains Indian prisoners first registered. Somehow there was a residue of voices. A visage of the story. Not simplistic, but elemental. Plain as the southwestern Oklahoma landscape. It was the kind of *voices* I picked up as *overlay* when I traveled. I think it was where I began to recognize the dislocation at the heart of education, especially Native education.

I found an early note from research. It was written with my typewriter before I had a computer—maybe it was when I was at the museum. "This piece of paper represents the earth. There is a big water all around the earth. There is no place to hide because the water is all around."—Lone Wolf, Kiowa, Fort Sill, Oklahoma, 1873. But I notice the date, 1873. The dates of the Fort Marion imprisonment were 1875–78. The words of Lone Wolf sound as if they were written after he had been at Fort Marion. Was the date wrong? Had I made an error in copying it? I was not able to find the source of Lone Wolf's quote. But I could see Lone Wolf sitting at the table in the casement with his ledger book. "This piece of paper represents the earth." But it should have been dated 1875. How would Lone Wolf have known about the water before he went to the ocean? Was it a prophetic statement? Was the piece of paper a treaty that he knew from experience was worthless? How could I reconcile the problem? How often writing about history discovers mystery rather than clarity.

The prisoners felt the train beneath them. They were chained to the walls. They rode sitting up. No one said anything. They could not have heard one another if they did. The train stopped at various places. The people were there to look at them. Word must have gone out that they were coming. How did they know? The U.S. Army had ways of communicating, but the wires for telegraph did not run everywhere. Maybe riders went ahead. Somehow they signaled because there was a crowd wherever they stopped. People gawked at them. Gray Beard was furious. He wanted to leap on the crowd. He wanted to jump the soldiers. But he would be killed.

What migration path did the train follow? How did they make the tracks that wandered across the land?

The new people came without rest. They marked the land. The prisoners had killed the surveyors. Some of them. There was no way to kill them all—to send them back. Where had the new people come from?—the Indians asked at council fires. The new people had come from a place far away. They had crossed the great waters. Now they crossed land. The Indians had to fight for the land and their lives. It's why they were now prisoners.

There were stories that the buffalo had gone inside the Wichita Mountains near Fort Sill in Indian Territory. The thunder and their voices had been one. The Indians would have followed them into the darkness inside the mountain. They were nothing without the buffalo.

The prisoners thought the soldiers would kill them. It seemed like they were taking them far away so that word would not get back to their tribes. The soldiers couldn't kill the prisoners in front of their families, though they had killed that way before. But the soldiers didn't kill them. The prisoners rode day after day until they reached a large fort made of stone. The soldiers all dressed alike. They had no difference in their clothes. No marks of bravery, except a few stripes on their clothes. They followed their leader—the one with the horn. It sounded in the morning and they were up, running, marching everywhere. The horn sounded again and they went to bed.

Captain Pratt cut the prisoners' hair and dressed them in army uniforms. He sat them in chairs at a table. Captain Pratt gave them ledger books. At first they drew to remember. But then drawing became an act of memory. They remembered because they drew.

The prisoners had been trouble causers. The soldiers sent them on a train to the great waters to get rid of them. To send them as far away from their people and land as they could. If the Indians at Fort Sill had no leaders, they would be easier to manage. What ideas could they have on their own? Or if they had ideas, they would not be able to act.

The soldiers called the great waters *ocean*. The prisoners knew it was where they were—a place where the water held its ceremonial dance.

Bear's Heart—I dreamed they tied a pencil to my hand. I dreamed they tied the ocean to our beds.

Drawing was now their war. The past brought regret and sadness because it was far away. They remembered the cries of their families as they left. How could they draw what they heard?

Tourists came to the fort to look at the prisoners. They stared when the Indians walked in town with Captain Pratt. The prisoners polished sea beans. They sold their drawings to the tourists.

Black Horse had his wife, Pe-ah-in, and his child, Ah-kes, because they had jumped into the wagon as it left Fort Sill. Where were the wives and children of the other prisoners? Would they be taken by others? Would the prisoners see them again? Would the land be there when they returned? Would they return?

Why had the new people come? What council had they sat in? Look at their wagons going farther across the land. Look at their towns where the prisoners stopped. The new people had buildings that could not be moved. They stood as a buffalo herd without legs, as teepees that could not be folded up and moved.

Buffalo Hunt, Bear's Heart, Ledger Book Drawing.
National Museum of the American Indian,
Smithsonian Institution (D206231).

The Animal Show

The prisoners complained—soldiers massacred Cheyenne and Arapaho families at Sand Creek. They massacred Black Kettle's people at the Washita River. The warriors had ridden the plains killing settlers and land surveyors. Did they think the new people would leave?—Just turn around and backtrack across the land? The prisoners heard other prisoners talking in their own languages, but it was the same story—

November 29, 1864—Seven hundred men from the Colorado Territory militia attacked Indian villages at Sand Creek in southeast Colorado Territory, mutilating many of the Indians, including women and children.

November 27, 1868—Colonel George Custer attacked an Indian village along the Washita River in Indian Territory. Previous to that, the Indians had signed the 1867 Medicine Lodge Treaty, which required the southern Cheyenne and Arapaho to move from Kansas and Colorado south into Indian Territory. In the summer of 1868 war parties from the Cheyenne, Arapaho, Kiowa, Comanche, Brule, Oglala Lakota, and Pawnee attacked settlers in western Kansas and southeastern Colorado. After that, it was a further flurry of treaties, skirmishes, massacres. It was war again.

And what came from it?—Defeat. Removal from the land they had known. Blindness as to where they were going. The unknown emptiness ahead of them. The loss behind them. It was beginning to dawn.

How does anyone unknot the strands? Unfold the layers? Surrender to history? Drive back with its intent in their thoughts? What is the retrieval process?—To restore voice to an event when the stirring of voices usually comes without names attached to them.

How does anyone present the different versions of the story, the subversions and verisimilitudes that come through travel and research? The different versions of the story—sometimes picking up loose ideas like threads.

———————

The few members of Making Medicine's family he had left watched from a distance as he walked to the wagon in chains that night at Fort Sill in Indian Territory. It had been dark, but he knew they were there. He thought about them as the prisoners jostled in the wagons. They rode with their heads bowed. For several days the wagons tossed over the rough ground. The ride was uncomfortable. The prisoners were stiff. Their bones ached. In Caddo they boarded the train. It was fear that captured them. It settled in the corners of any space they found. It came over them like brush fire. Their hearts were animals running from the flames.

———————

I'm interested in different versions of the same story—the telling and retelling of the story in different ways—moving from third person to first and back. It's how multiple retellings seem to work. It's how I heard the prisoners' voices—their voice fragments. I wanted the multiple narrators—the rewrite of a broken history broken into different narratives. I wanted the many versions it takes to tell a story. What was said on the surface—what was thought underneath. I tried to work between the unfolding versions of history.

———————

The train stopped with a jerk. The soldiers pushed back the door—unlocked their chains from the wall—pulled the prisoners into the air. The Indians were murderers—savages of the plains. The people stared at them. Maybe the people wondered if the prisoners were even human.

AH-KES, THE DAUGHTER OF BLACK HORSE—The light hurts my eyes.

BLACK HORSE—Stay between your mother and me, Ah-kes.

BIG NOSE—I dreamed horses were talking to the sky. They were telling it to stay awake. The enemy was coming. The horses didn't talk with words—but with their snorting.

CHIEF KILLER—Maybe the train was telling the sky something.

HU-WAH-NEE—The train didn't know how to talk to the sky. It was an animal that pulled the wagons.

The prisoners were given a drink of water from a dipper—then loaded on the train and chained to the wall again. The door was closed. The train continued.

Ta-a-way-te's legs felt full of creek water.

Buffalo Meat felt his heart in his wrists and ankles. He felt his heart throbbing under the iron ropes. He had more than one heart beating—*Aaaaeeee!*

SKY WALKER—*Shuuuu*, there are others riding with us—others we can't see. Not because of the darkness—but because they were from another world. Think of them—they will hold our hearts—all of us—

Ta-a-way-te slept chained to the wall with his head on his chest until he couldn't raise his head. His neck yowled with stiffness. He cried with leg cramps. His legs slept until they tingled as if wolves ate them.

MATCHES—When the soldiers opened the door of the rail car, they had to pull Ta-a-way-te out. He couldn't walk. His toes moved like warriors. They told a story—his toes had been shot with arrows.

Black Horse pushed the soldiers away. He would help Ta-a-way-te walk. The soldiers pushed back. Someone struck—the soldiers ordered the prisoners to the ground. They sat huddled together until everyone was quiet. Then the soldiers ordered them to their feet again. Some of the soldiers pulled a few of the prisoners to their feet again—the ones who had trouble standing.

They walked through the streets where people gathered to watch them pass. The prisoners entered the fort behind the soldiers who walked with Ta-a-way-te between them.

BIG MOCCASIN—What were these stone walls we walked through? What was this damp air—this smell?—What was all that water beyond?—

AH-KES—Where's the land?—

BLACK HORSE—Under the water.

AH-KES—How do you know?

BLACK HORSE—The land holds everything—even this—

PE-AH-IN, THE WIFE OF BLACK HORSE—But what was it?—One sky facing another?

BIG NOSE—It's the ocean.

MANIMIC—The great waters—the place the soldiers came from.

WHITE BEAR—It smells like something dead.

LONE WOLF—The ocean is at war with the land. Look at it trying to climb on the land. It attacks and attacks—

STRAIGHTENING AN ARROW—The ocean is a prisoner, like us—

BEAR'S HEART—Hear it rumble—

TA-A-WAY-TE—It makes noise like the train.

PE-AH-IN—How can we know the water?—This place of no use.

TA-A-WAY-TE—What can we do with water? Could we ride a horse on it?

LONE WOLF—I knew it was here before I came.

BLACK HORSE—It is troubled—tossing—tossing.

PE-AH-IN—How can we stay here?

AH-KES—Hey, Ocean—be quiet out there—

BLACK HORSE—A trouble causer—like us.

PE-AH-IN—How can we live by this water?

BLACK HORSE—I don't think the soldiers will let us go back.

AH-KES—Why?

BLACK HORSE—The Indians broke the soldiers' laws.

AH-KES—But they aren't the Indians' laws—

In the night Black Horse heard the moaning of the prisoners—the whimpering of Pe-ah-in, his wife—the crying of Ah-kes, his daughter. He heard the pleading of others. Black Horse gritted his teeth—this darkness would not get them.

In the night Pe-ah-in held her hand over her nose. The smell did not go away. The walls were damp. They were like touching an animal that had been skinned.

The Morning Had a Bugle
in Its Mouth

When Captain Richard Henry Pratt, chief at Fort Marion, dressed the prisoners as soldiers, he walked them around the fort. They had military drills—and discipline. Some of the prisoners struggled with the soldiers. They did not want to do what they were told. Many of them were taken to a small dark windowless room. They had to bend down to enter. Ta-a-way-te and the others were quiet when they came back.

Captain Pratt gave the prisoners ledger books the fort used to keep accounts. He gave them drawing sticks. They opened the ledger books and drew horses and buffalo hunts.

Didn't Captain Pratt know they could draw?—Hadn't he see their teepee drawings? Hide paintings? Winter counts? Rock paintings? Pratt had been in Indian Territory. Maybe Captain Pratt and the soldiers were too busy hunting the Indians to know much about them.

Why didn't Pratt know the Indians found ledger books left by soldiers marking their trade—and books marked with their names that Kicking Bird and other informants had given them?

Standing Wolf limped during military drills. It was an old wound—stealing horses from a soldiers' camp. Captain Pratt let Standing Wolf sit when he could not walk. There were days he stayed in the infirmary—cramped with pain. Making Medicine prayed for him at night. But there was no gourd rattle. There was no medicine song in this new place.

Each morning, Standing Wolf felt the sound of the bugle in his leg.

Night

It was the hardest to be away from their people after dark. At night on the rack bed together, they almost could hear them. At night they listened to the breath of one another. Now it was Toothless snoring. No—it was Howling Wolf. Ah-kes made little snorts to mock them. The men who tried to sleep laughed at her noises. How could they sleep? On the prairie sound traveled between the teepees, but it dissipated into the air. In the casement at Fort Marion, where they all slept in one room, the walls held the noise.

Snrzzz, Ah-kes said. *SNUURZ.*

Ah-kes, her mother said, and Ah-kes was quiet.

In the silence they could hear someone sing a song. Not loud, but enough of a sound they knew the song. They could hear it between the snorings. They could sing sometimes without noise. The song would be in their minds. They could hear it in the others. They all joined in the song.

It was in the song that they heard the pecking. It was the old story that stayed with them—when their people lived in a hollow cottonwood waiting for release. An owl pecked a hole, and the Indians emerged. It was the same darkness in the casement where they slept. An owl would come. They could hear the pecking.

No—it was Toothless snoring, Black Horse said, and laughter followed.

In the morning Black Horse told his wife he had been on the prairie in the night—when he finally got to sleep. But Pe-ah-in told him he was dreaming.

Was it when you were asleep, or when you listened to the buffalo grunting?

No, Black Horse answered. He was there. He heard the wind in the cottonwoods.

It was only the ocean, Pe-ah-in insisted.

He heard an animal lapping Horse Creek in the dark, he said.

Yes, Manimic agreed. He could still see the land.

Digging a Hole in the Water

Sky Walker stood on the wall at the fort. He remembered when he was on the prairie riding his horse. He killed settlers and whoever did not belong there. He killed his enemies. That's what a warrior did. He shot them with his arrows. He bludgeoned them with his tomahawk. He scalped. He burned. But the cavalry had weapons bigger than his. Guns. Repeating rifles. Cannons. You can imagine how the Indians could not fight against the soldiers. The Indians held a council. They argued. They talked. They mourned their sacred land and their way of life. They surrendered, riding to Fort Sill near the Wichita Mountains with their white flag. The land was called Indian Territory, but the soldiers said it was theirs. The land surveyors said the same. And the settlers. The soldiers built a fort. They shot the buffalo. Sky Walker's children cried with hunger.

SKY WALKER—I tell you we had visions of everything toppling on its side.

_____

I listened to Keith Richards's book *Life*, recently when I traveled. As I neared the end of another draft in what seemed an endless exploration of how to write the prisoners' voices, I saw his audio book in the library.

Richards's life was a life of privilege that came from music. Most of it I fast forwarded, which was the same route he took, his on drugs, mine on the button on the car radio. But when he talked about his creative endeavors in music, he was right on. His "melancholy dissonance" resonated with the dissonant music of the prisoners' journey and imprisonment.

Richards also talked about the mix, the throw-ins—"an amalgamation, a mangling and a dangling and a tangling thing. There is no 'properly.'"

Yet it was the impossible *properly* I searched for in the writing of the Fort Marion voices.

———————

The soldiers sent the Indians away after they surrendered. What else was there to do with them? The Indians saw the train tracks people built. They saw the rail cars that could go over the land. The soldiers put the Indians into the cars and chained them to the wall. The train went faster than a horse riding into battle. It made noise. Sometimes steam came in a little roof window like ghosts in their visions.

The ghosts rode the train with them. They were like the smoke from campfires. Or the fog on Medicine Creek on a winter morning. No—the ghosts came from the train—ghosts tall as the air streaming above the train. It was a ghost-house moving on wheels. That's what the soldiers had—wheels—That's why the settlers rolled into their land. That's why they rolled over their hunting grounds.

The prisoners rode for days. The train went one way. The train went another way. It stopped. It started again. Others rode with them—Thunder Beings—Flying Beings with their foreheads painted black.

Each day the Indians went farther away from the prairie and their land near the Wichita Mountains in Indian Territory. Each day they heard their relatives. The cries of their children. The voices came to them on the wind. They knew they were alive. They sent word back to them that they were still alive. The birds would take their message to their relatives. Their voices would reach their land near Fort Sill. Their families would be given rations and would survive. Most of them anyway, those who would not die of a broken heart—or the illnesses that the settlers brought. Why didn't the settlers die of their own spotted disease? Their coughing disease? Sometimes they did. But mostly they survived.

Boarding the Steam Boat in Jacksonville on the Way to St. Augustine, Bear's Heart, Ledger Book Drawing. National Museum of the American Indian, Smithsonian Institution (D20623I).

Backtrack

Gray Beard crawled from the train window in chains just before night. The train backed to the spot where Gray Beard had disappeared in the palmetto forest of northern Florida. Soldiers followed with lanterns, and soon the prisoners heard their shots.

Later that night they heard the Spirit Beings—the Thunder Beings that traveled with the train. Gray Beard rode with them now.

When the prisoners saw the ocean, they had to have been afraid. What was it?—Water. More water than the land they had come from—more restless than the tall grasses on the prairie. *Even the waves had wheels*—see them rolling onto the shore. Listen to the Thunder Beings pound their drum!

The fear that met them at the train station in Caddo, Indian Territory, was there at the boat dock in Florida. What was the object that sat on the water like a toad? It was big as a village. But there was no land under it. There were no tracks for it to run on. How could they get into it? Was this where the soldiers would kill them? The toad would swallow them and the water would swallow the toad. Pe-ah-in and Ah-kes trembled against Black Horse. He was afraid also. Everyone was. How could they trust the object to carry them like a horse? But the soldiers got on the boat. They didn't think they would drown. The prisoners had no choice but to be herded onto the boat. The steam boat, it was called. A talking village that walked on water.

At Fort Marion the prisoners cut off the legs of the military trousers the soldiers gave them and used the fabric for leggings to go with their breech-cloths.

At the fort Captain Pratt give the prisoners ledger books and told them to draw. The Indians were record keepers. Now their winter counts were drawn in lined books instead of on teepee hides. Howling Wolf drew their horses on the prairie. He drew the train to Florida. He left the corners of the ledger book open for the ghosts and Thunder Beings.

The prisoners spoke different languages—Comanche, Kiowa, Arapaho, Kiowa, Caddo. Some of them couldn't understand one another except by sign language.

At Fort Marion women came and taught the prisoners their English language. Some of the Indians refused to learn. But if they learned their words, they could speak to one another.

Remember the letters that made treaties they could not read? Learn them so they would know what they say when they covered their voices with these marks—these rows of beaver-bone breast-plates. The soldiers' language was water. When the prisoners learned to write, they could dig a hole in the water.

May 24, 1875—Wolf Stomach, the brother of Toothless, died in the post hospital. He asked Toothless to cut their throats—Come to death with me. But Toothless refused. He dressed his brother in his old clothes, painting his face for his journey. They placed his body in a pine coffin, took him to the post cemetery, and buried him in the southeast corner because it was the soldiers' law. Toothless left his brother's tin cup by the grave and made a speech—With his cup, Wolf Stomach digs a hole in the water.

Making Medicine sat with the other prisoners in a casement with the window open. The warm air came in—The call of sea birds in the distance. They watched the teacher make marks on the chalk board. They followed her marks on our slate boards with their marks. See—this is the way the rain makes a rivulet in the dust. This is the way the clouds curl in the sky.

BEAR'S HEART—This is the way a snake coils when it is hurt. This is the way a young buffalo hops when it smells a storm.

ZOTOM—This is the way the wind turns back upon itself.

MAKING MEDICINE—This is the way we lost our hearts. This is the way we get them back.

The prisoners learned to speak their language. They learned to write. They heard the squeak of the chalk like the train on its track coming into the station at St. Augustine. Writing was slow as a train leaving the station to start on its track again. Writing was movement over the land. Sometimes writing was making letters that backtracked on themselves.

Zotom wrote his letters—ME GO.

The words were hard to learn. The letters in the words sat with others, changing the sound of those they sat by, and sometimes they were changed themselves. They were traitors, those letters. They were Indian scouts for the U.S. cavalry.

July 24, 1875—Lean Bear died from starvation. He had stabbed himself halfway through the journey from Indian Territory to Florida and had been left in a hospital in Nashville. When he recovered, he was sent to Fort Marion, but he chose not to survive.

It was always there—the distance from their land. The separation from their families. They suffered dysentery—and the heaviness that held them as if they were still shackled.

They washed the green scum from the walls of the fort. They listened as the missionaries read their Bible—Who can gather the wind in his fists?—Who has bound the water in a garment?[1]

Who can gather water in his fists?—Toothless asked—Who can dig a hole in the water?

The ministers continued to come to the fort. They taught the prisoners news of their God. He came to all people. He gave himself. He was food and shelter and life. The Indians thought they

1. Proverbs 30:4

meant the buffalo. The Indians knew him, they said—he came to them as an animal. Captain Pratt did not know what they meant.

The people walked in darkness, the ministers told them. Yes, the Indians knew the story of their origin. They were inside a tree. Walking around. Knocking over everything. Then they heard an owl pecking. And there was a hole and they walked out of the tree into this world. That pecking was the nails in the cross, they said, that brought them from dark to light. Yes, then they knew that story too.

Manimic said his children were hungry. He heard their voices in the gulls that circled overhead. He wanted to go back. The children didn't understand what happened. They didn't know an ocean. But they heard bits of it in the visions the prisoners sent.

July 29, 1875—Sky Walker died.

Captain Richard Henry Pratt decided the prisoners should govern themselves. He made a courtroom in one of the casements. A court of Indians convened. The accused heard the charges. After pleas and testimony on both sides, the court determined the verdict and penalty.

When Hail Stone stole a chicken, he brought it to the fort, flapping its wings, his hand over its beak to keep it from squeaking. He killed it, took its feathers for the small pow wows Captain Pratt allowed them to practice, calling them dance ceremonies—or *show dances*. The Indians, who wore eagle feathers for their ceremonies, had to use chicken feathers?

Then the man who owned the chicken came to the fort saying his chicken was gone.

Hail Stone appeared in court for a trial by jury. The jury of prisoners found Hail Stone guilty and sentenced him to eight days of confinement in the dark cell without bread or water. Richard Henry Pratt asked for retrial and bread and water were given.

The Indian court imposed severe sentences. Pratt didn't remember the different tribes had been enemies on the plains. He didn't know the meanness they felt toward one another. He didn't know they sentenced Hail Stone for thinking they would wear chicken feathers.

They had scouting expeditions to Mantanzas Inlet. They walked around the town. They bivouacked near Jack Mound and Anastasia Island. They pitched white canvas tents on a bluff overlooking the beach.

October 5, 1875—Straightening an Arrow died from consumption.

The prisoners marched. They fished and hunted. They had foot races. They collected sea shells and ate oysters. One day Big Nose left camp and disappeared with a non-Indian party of boaters. He was absent four hours. When he returned, he had to carry a heavy log around the courtyard of the fort for two hours. The other prisoners had to watch.

November 4, 1875—Big Moccasin died of uremic poisoning. The doctor found he had tied a string around his penis so he could not urinate.

The prisoners made bows and arrows and sold them in town. They polished sea beans and sold them. They sold alligator teeth. Tourists bought their ledger-book drawings. The prisoners sent money to their families in Indian Territory—

> Matches—mother $5.00
> Manimic—wife $10.00 and daughter $2.00
> Heap of Birds—wife $4.00
> Howling Wolf—wife $4.00 and friend $2.00
> Making Medicine—mother $6.00

The family of Making Medicine sent him moccasins and a deer-leg pipe.

December 5, 1876—Standing Wolf died from paralysis from an injury he suffered before he came. It was a stiffness-he-could-not-move-away-from.

January 2, 1877—Spotted Elk died of consumption.

The prisoners studied arithmetic. They learned numbers. Buffalo Meat made a chart of goods for sale at a St. Augustine merchant—ink 10 cts paper 20 cts shoes $2 shirts $1 cuffs 50 cts handkerchiefs 10 cts.

October 8, 1877—Heap of Birds died of congestion and heart disease.
    The Thunder Beings kept up their plowing on the shore.
    And what do we do with cuffs and a handkerchief?—Dry Wood asked. _____

November 5, 2011—I visited the post cemetery, which is now St. Augustine National Cemetery, several blocks from the fort. I found the two white upright stones, 339 and 340, that read "6 Unknown Indians." I left an offering of Cuba's finest tobacco, which I bought at the Cuban Corner Cigar Company just off the square in St. Augustine. The twelve left their bodies there. Who knows where their spirits went?

Chart of Goods for Sale, Buffalo Meat, Ledger Book Drawing. Yale Collection of Western Americana, Beinecke Rare Book and Manuscript Library.

To Mrs Marion Jennings
Mothers sister. M.P.S.

Dear Marion

I send you
Buffalo Meats price
current or mem-
of price of such
things as the Indians
want to buy in town
I discovered it in
a book of memoranda
he keeps and had
him copy for me
since which he
has been busy making
copies for the winter.
Quite amusing, I
think

Henry

The Ax in My Hand

Bear's Heart and E-tah-dle-uh drew the military drills in their ledger books—this was how the soldiers came into their land, with their numbers, their ranks, their precision. Indian warfare sometimes was counting coup—touching their enemy and riding away. Other times the Indians killed and dismembered. They moved in the spirit when they rode into war.

Let the soldiers give the Indians guns to go with those military drills they did each day in the square courtyard of Fort Marion—

It was Chivington at Sand Creek and Custer at Washita in the Black Kettle Grasslands. They rode into the Indian camps—killed their families. After that, the cottonwoods began to leave. After that, the Indians were the disrupters of telegraph wires. They were horse thieves, raiders of wagon trains, murderers of settlers and government surveyors who marked off their buffalo hunting grounds.

They rode as warriors. They defended themselves. They wanted to keep their land. They tried to keep the soldiers from running over them. Yes, E-tah-dle-uh still could feel that ax in his hand.

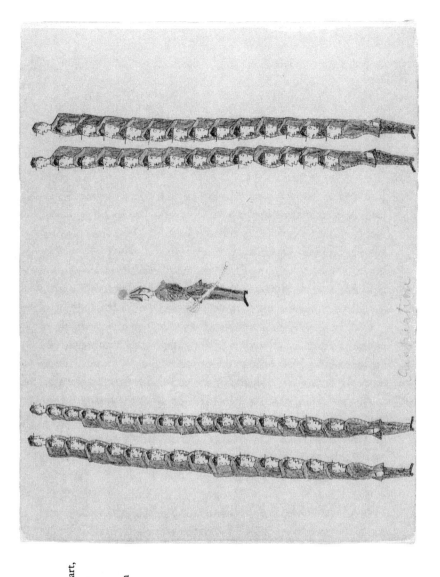

Military Formation at Fort Marion, Bear's Heart, Ledger Book Drawing. National Museum of the American Indian, Smithsonian Institution (D20623r).

Fort Marion

Fort Marion was named Castillo de San Marcos when Spaniards began construction in 1672. When the British occupied the fort from 1763 to 1784, they called it Fort St. Mark. In 1821, when Florida became U.S. territory, the Americans named it Fort Marion, after a hero from the Revolutionary War. Osceola and other Seminoles were imprisoned there before the Plains Indians. In 1942 the name was returned to the original Castillo de San Marcos.

Fort Marion is a square structure with thick walls made of coquina, a pale, nearly white sedimentary rock that consists of crushed shells. Inside the structure, casements, or rooms, line an open courtyard. On one side of the courtyard, there's a staircase to the terreplein, a walkway inside the wall of the fort above the casements. On the four corners of the terreplein are large triangular bastions called ravelins. Along the terreplein are embrasures in the walls where cannons face outward to the sea and the surrounding land.

When I visited the fort, I walked through the casements where the classrooms were held. I looked at the platform beds where they slept side by side. I crawled into the inner room with no windows and a small door that possibly served as the cell for confinement. Outside, I climbed the stairs again and stood on the wall in the wind and the noise of the air. I stood on the bastions at the four corners of the fort. I heard the gulls overhead. I smelled the ocean. I saw the lighthouse across Matanzas Bay on Anastasia Island. I felt the distance from where I traveled, taking notes on the small, far away voices tucked in the corners of the casements. The rooms had doors rounded at the top. They reminded me of the cellar with its pounded earth floor on my grandparents' farm.

In an old photograph of Osceola, imprisoned at the fort in 1837 after the Second Seminole War, he looks out from between the bars of his cell. There is no longer a recognizable cell at the fort, but faint imprints can be found above the door on one of the casements, ghost-marks of prison bars.

I always feel a story of Native history in my throat. It begins with a tightening there—I think because of the loss.

Little evidence remains of the Indians at Fort Marion. There are a few wall drawings in a few of the casements, almost indiscernible, which Gail Slemmer called graffiti in her *Interpretive Plan*. The petroglyphs are slowly disappearing. They are visages of animals and warriors. They remain an act of placing what is known upon the unknown.

The voices of the prisoners were just as faded when I began to hear them.

I have sat on the steps at Fort Marion. I have looked at the ocean.

Ledger Book Drawings (1)

Bear's Heart thought if he held his breath, he would die. He would leave the ocean and return to the prairie. But Captain Richard Henry Pratt sat Bear's Heart in a chair. He gave him a ledger book. He gave him a drawing stick. He placed the prisoner's hand around it. He moved it in the book. Bear's Heart pulled his hand away. He drew by himself. He thought about the prairie. He made marks with the drawing sticks. He floated through the air. The drawing sticks were his wings. They were magic sticks. A horse came from the stick. It crossed the land from the prairie. Bear's Heart make another drawing—and another. The drawings were horses. He rode upon them. He heard them at night. In his dreams the horses ran.

Reports from the prisoners—

E-TAH-DLE-UH—Captain Pratt brought the tourists to see us. The tourists bought our drawings.

HE-WAH-NEE—Captain Pratt made us polish alligator teeth for tourists.

BLACK HORSE—I am a warrior of the plains, now I weave palm hats.

TA-A-WAY-TE—My alligator teeth sell more than your hats.

AH-KES—The shells were small teepees from the ocean.

PE-AH-IN—Did some of them go under the water—when they died?

BLACK HORSE—Maybe the bad ones—the ones who were traitors—the ones who led the soldiers to us.

AH-KES—But weren't they the ones in prison? Weren't they the bad ones—?

BLACK HORSE—They were bad to the soldiers, but not to themselves.

AH-KES—What was bad? What did we do?

BLACK HORSE—The Indian's bad was not bad to us. The soldiers' bad was not bad to them—but their bad was bad to us, and the Indians' bad was bad to the soldiers.

The Life Casts

Captain Pratt asked Clark Mills to come to Fort Marion from Washington to make life casts of the Indians' heads. Mills would cover their faces with plaster, he told them. Maybe they thought it would be as dark as the inside of the mountains where the buffalo went.

How did Captain Pratt get the Indians to sit for the plaster casts of their heads and necks?—What did he say to make them agree? Did he tell them they would go to the cell without windows? Did he say he would not give them letters from their families?

I imagine he probably told each of them something different. He knew the reward or punishment he would inflict—whatever they most wanted or feared.

Captain Pratt had his own cast made first. The Indians lined up in the casement to see if Pratt would die. They watched him sit in a chair. A muslin sheet was tucked into the neck of his shirt—his hair under a cap. Clark Mills plastered the captain's head, his neck, his ears, his face. There were small reeds in his nose to breathe. The Indians' hearts must have beat fast as they watched. When the plaster hardened, Mills cracked it in a few places with a small hammer. He removed the pieces and put them back together—and there was a likeness of Captain Pratt's head.

It made them shiver to see the ghost-head—

They went into the room. One at a time. They come out silent. This underwater breathing—this smothering. These cylinders in their nose and mouth for air.

Ah-kes did not want to go. But her father told her to come with him—he would talk to her the way a horse talks. He would nibble the grass in her hand.

She sat by her father as Mills put stoppers in his ears. Black Horse closed his eyes. Mills put small cylinders in his nose and mouth so he could breathe. Ah-kes knew he was afraid. He did not flinch the way a horse does when you take its mane. He spoke the way a horse spoke without words. Black Horse did not move as Mills covered his face and head with plaster. He was quieter than a horse. And braver. Slowly, slowly, Ah-kes felt his finger draw a horse in her palm—a horse no one could see. Slowly, slowly, the horse nibbled the grass she held for him.

Now it was her turn—she sat beside her father though she didn't want plaster on her face.

Black Horse told her to think of a horse all her own. A small, small horse that she could keep behind her ear. It was the horse she would have had if they had been on the prairie. It would tell her a story she could hear even with her ears covered.

Ah-kes reminded Black Horse that their horses had been killed—

Black Horse told her that they would be the stories the horses would have told if they had not been killed. The stories of prairie wind. Of grass fires. Of stars hunting.

What did the stars hunt for? Ah-kes asked.

Black Horse answered, the sun, of course—they would always find it. Had she ever had two nights together without light between them?

Yes, she reminded her father—when we were in the box-that-rides.

Yes, he said, but they knew light was outside the rail car. They could hear the light say, I am here. They just couldn't see it.

Ah-kes said she didn't hear the light talk.

But Black Horse said he did. Now sit there while the man covers your face and feel the horse nibble at your hand.

When the plaster was on Manimic's face, he was in the darkness inside the Wichita Mountains. He could hear the buffalo standing with him—waiting for the return of the Indians.

When the plaster was on Ta-a-way-te's face, he had a vision. He was shut in the box-that-walks again. It turned upside down.

There were others with him—he was suffocating. Ta-a-way-te flailed, but they held his arms until he stopped. Mills and Pratt assured him it wouldn't last long. In Ta-a-way-te's vision, he was falling. There were others with their arms uplifted to catch him. They looked as if they had been made with drawing sticks on a ledger book. The light shone through them. Those receiving them were in another world. Was Ta-a-way-te dreaming his death? His birth?

When he closed his eyes under the gauze, he saw the darkness inside the box-that-walked that brought them there. When he closed his eyes, he saw bodies in a heap. They were Indians who were dead. The Indians left some of theirs in the grave too—that's what counted now to Ta-a-way-te.

Mills took so long to make Ta-a-way-te's cast he felt a hand on his shoulder. It was Captain Pratt. He heard his voice. He was sorry, he was sorry, he said. He knew what it was to be under plaster.

Hu-wah-nee clenched his teeth when the plaster was on his face. He held as still as a wolf while it waits for its prey.

Chief Killer wanted to kill them. He had been one who told others what to do. Now he followed the soldiers' rules because he didn't want to be in the dark cell—he didn't want to live this way. He wanted to be as he was before.

Manimic wanted to pick up that train, turn it around, head it back the way it came.

Buffalo Meat told Manimic he would never ride that train again. He still had the marks of shackles on his ankles.

Howling Wolf would ride the train again, if it left the ocean.

Making Medicine sat in a chair waiting for the plaster of the cast. The man whose name was Clark Mills plugged his ears. He placed hollow sticks in Making Medicine's nose and mouth. The others had told him how it felt—he would think Mills was going to kill him—but Mills would not. Making Medicine felt the plaster spread across his forehead, his cheeks, his nose, his mouth, chin, neck. He was alone inside himself. Everything he knew was gone. His eyes stung—they were wet. The eye coverings kept his eyes from showing. No one would see him cry. Making Medicine was breaking—yet he held himself still with resolve. This was what he chose—under the plaster of this cast, the stillness was with him. A voice was there—God was his name. The Maker's new name—did the Maker change his name? Didn't Indians change their names? He argued.

What would he write to his friends?—There was an ocean on his head? Making Medicine heard the voice of God—the Maker—though his ears were plugged. Didn't he hear it in Christian education? The Maker God came—he too was hated—he too was sent away—Making Medicine's heart lifted into his, became his—how could he say it?—There was a being there inside the plaster with him.

Now it was E-tah-dle-uh's turn—Mills told him to close his eyes. They plugged his ears. They put cylinders in his nose and mouth. They placed gauze over his head and face. He felt he was in thickets so overgrown he could never climb out.

Then Mills covered Dry Wood's face with plaster. Dry Wood was shaking with fear. Pratt held him in the chair. *Breathe,* Pratt said. Dry Wood had fallen in a creek when he was a boy. He couldn't breathe. Now he was under water again. His father's hand grabbed his arm. He heard the pecking of the small hammer on the cast. It was his father pulling him out. No, it was the old story of the owl—pecking, pecking, letting the people out.

Photograph, Fort Marion Casts, Peabody Museum, Harvard
University photograph. Courtesy of the Peabody Museum of
Archaeology and Ethnology, Harvard University [2013.0.3]
#99030091.

The Process of Writing (1)

WB: *Are you ever tempted to compose works again in traditional form?*
JC: *Yes, of course, but I think it is my responsibility to resist such*
    temptation.

WAYNE BOOTH, *For the Love of It: Amateuring and Its Rivals*

I wanted to write about the Fort Marion prisoners once I saw their
plaster casts or life masks in storage in the Peabody Museum at
Harvard University in the summer of 2005. They were made by the
sculptor Clark Mills, who made the statue of Andrew Jackson in
Lafayette Square in Washington DC. Richard Henry Pratt asked
Mills to come to Fort Marion to make casts of the *vanishing race.*

A friend, Jackie Old Coyote, told me about the masks. One
summer, when I was at a workshop at Bard College in New York,
I drove to Cambridge, Massachusetts, to meet Jackie and Patricia Capone, associate curator of the Peabody. I found my way
onto the Harvard campus. I found the Peabody Museum. Park-
ing is impossible on a university campus, but I remember there
was a place for my car directly in front of the Peabody. Inside the
museum Patricia Capone took us upstairs to the archives. She
opened the large double doors. We walked in. She turned on the
lights. There on the shelves were the casts. They sat in rows as if
they still were in the schoolroom. I could see the expressions on
their faces. The muscles tight along the jaw. The faces afraid or
defiant or passive. I felt their voices in my throat. It was more
like a lump in my throat. I felt their stories wanting to be told. I
felt their words wanting out.

Afterward their voices rode with me. Or maybe I rode with them. I would be somewhere in the present, and an image or visage would come from the past.

When I taught at Kenyon College in 2008–2009, I attended a concert by a young Cuban pianist. He was an experimental musician, opening the lid of the piano, pounding on the wires, on the keys, on the piano itself. In the clacking rhythm and momentum of sound, I was on the train to St. Augustine, Florida. Through the whole concert, I rode with the prisoners from Fort Sill, Indian Territory, to Fort Marion, Florida.

At the Cummer Museum in Jacksonville, Florida, on my way to St. Augustine on one of the research trips, I saw an exhibit called A Kiowa's Odyssey: A Sketchbook from Fort Marion, consisting of E-tah-dle-uh's ledger book drawings. The drawings were one of the main occupations at Fort Marion. They are statements of alignment—trying to re-find balance. Some of the drawings were titled *The Night of Surrender, Indian Prisoners Arriving at Caddo, Crossing the Mississippi at St. Louis, The Arrival in Nashville, A Trip to Matanzas 16 Miles South of St. Augustine, Killing Buffalo,* and *Young Kiowas Dressed for a Ceremonial Visit.* The two-room gallery was filled with the colored pencil on paper drawings.

Richard Henry Pratt, who had been in charge of the Indian prisoners at Fort Marion, had typed his comments and interpretations above the drawings. A note explained that Pratt's typewritten captions were added to the drawings about 1920: "Though informative, they fundamentally changed the original condition of the drawings." Pratt took the actual pages on which the drawings were penciled and typed on them. I was horrified at first that someone would do that—but then I had the thought of conflation—combining variant texts—story by story—I thought of how I could combine their story with my own story of finding their story. I could use both the story of the Fort Marion prisoners and my own story of the process of writing their voices.

This is the problem—the fragments—flying fragments of history scattered by the wind—picked up along the road during travel—and stopping by the shore. Imagined words of the prisoners shuffled into the nonfiction of the event—mine as well as theirs—with voices often choppy as the waves. Each layer a new development with so many versions that the truth lies somewhere in the spaces between them. Or in the versions bound together overriding the text riding above like clouds, or the truth of the sea broken into various incoming waves. It is what happens anyway as I travel. I only had to be responsible for the way the voices appeared to me.

It was in school I became an outsider to myself. It was where I learned I would endure. The lessons there were that I was alone. My father had come to Kansas City for work—where there was no one of our kind. School. School. Uncomfortable school. The repetition of it every year.

This is the lesson that falls back upon itself like waves.

———————

I long for road trips. Days of traveling alone. On a 2008 spring break I drove from Gambier, Ohio, to Rhome, Texas, northwest of Fort Worth to visit family, and then to St. Augustine and Jacksonville, Florida, for research, and back to Gambier.

In Mississippi on my way from Texas to Florida I passed along the coastal highway in the wake of Hurricane Katrina. I stopped in Biloxi and Bay St. Louis. Much of the rubble had been cleared, but in Bay St. Louis I stopped to pick up a brick for the collection of rocks I keep at my cabin in the Ozarks—and there in the bay I saw a train on a long trestle bridge crossing the water. It was small in the distance—small as the train that carried the Indian prisoners to Fort Marion in 1875.

A slight purple wash covered the sky—from the slant of the low sun on the Gulf—or the uncertainty of the water that reflected its light. The air seemed amethyst. The sky was clear, but faded by a haze in late afternoon. Maybe the memory has a purple wash over it. The remembering of the remembering.

I thought I could hear the train in the distance—the repetition of the devotions of the train on its track—the rhythmic passing of the cars.

At my son's place in Texas, a train passes in the night a half mile from his house. Even the baby wakes and talks to the noise and then returns to sleep.

At Fort Marion the Indian prisoners received the gift of pencils that made color. At Fort Marion they received the amethyst air.

On that 2008 trip I left Mobile early in the morning. It was afternoon before I neared the east coast of Florida. What was up? I looked at the map. It was four hundred miles on I-10 across northern Florida from Alabama to Jacksonville, then forty miles south on I-95 to St. Augustine. I knew it was four hundred miles across Kansas; North and South Dakota also. I hadn't realized that all of Florida was not a narrow strip of land between the Atlantic Ocean and the Gulf of Mexico.

At the rest stop I also discovered how much like Missouri Alabama looks—two upright states, or nearly so, with boot heels, Alabama's on the west, Missouri's on the east. (Louisiana is the boot shape itself.) Look at Mississippi also. I closed the map and drove on before I made an unnecessary study of the shape of geography in my atlas.

It is on the road—with my file box strapped into the front seat, with its research notes and books and beginnings of the writing—that I find distinctive structures or rough architecture for the writing, something like the shapes of the pastel states I've crossed. A piece of nonfiction (or any writing for that matter) usually begins with an empty place, something like the pale blue water on the map surrounding Florida. I only have 440 miles to go before I find some of the strings that will hold the story together.

In all my travels I have known that voices from the past haunt the land where they happened. They leave small demarcation lines.

Their visages are still there. At my lowest, I think they are part of an ongoing human endeavor—wiping out those who can be wiped out, or at least moved over—though they themselves are the ones that were wiped out—or nearly. But the Indians were at war with the Indians long before the white man came. Tribal warfare is as long as Indian history.

Every time I enter my small cabin on the Lake of the Ozarks in Missouri, there are remnants of war on the floor. I sweep up the bodies of small bugs that have been sucked dry by spiders hiding in the walls. Everything must eat, I suppose. From insects to black holes. These issues clamp onto me like the fierce patches of poison ivy that I caught recently on a walk in the woods and now cover my arms, legs, and neck.

These are small voices swept under the greater injustices—the global injustices of cruel regimes and ethnic cleansings. If I begin to list them, they would obliterate the small voices in this book. Already they sweep over these American voices, or the voices from the New America when it was putting its foot down across the continent, saying to the wilderness, the buffalo, the Indians who lived there: this is the way it will be.

I am interested in giving voice to those marked with the long and sometimes cruel history of Indian education, which usually was tied to Christian education.

I want to *set right* a small part of America's history by recognizing the stains on America's self-appointed clean self-image. In Genesis 4:10 there's an interesting passage—"The voice of your brother's blood cries to me from the ground." It's these voices I hear driving over the ground of America in my *wafty* process of retrieving voices from the land.

The same is said again in Isaiah 26:21—"The earth will disclose the blood shed upon her." Did the missionaries not know their own words? Or the words of the God who sent them when they came to move us over so they could settle on our land?—Though they preached it was their heavenly land we were to enter, and they would move over for us.

Didn't they know the land would record the stains they caused?

The Ocean Dogs

Each day at Fort Marion there were a few tasks. *Routine* was a word the prisoners soon learned. Each day the sameness weighed upon them. Sometimes their memory of the plains was like the rise and fall of the ocean. But even that had a sameness. If they wove their tasks with stories, maybe they would survive. If they saw the ocean changing the way the prairie changed—but the sameness of the ocean overwhelmed their stories with its sameness.

Roar—Roar. Pe-ah-in stood with Ah-kes and Black Horse on the wall of the fort. Below them a few soldiers fished. Some of the prisoners had joined them. Pe-ah-in turned away from the wall and looked at the sky when she heard Ah-kes's voice. The other prisoners watching from the wall shouted also.

AH-KES—What's gulping on the shore below us?

THE PRISONERS—A water dog?—An ocean dog?—What did the soldiers call it?—The large fish they pull in?—

The prisoners shaded their eyes against the brightness. The noise of wind, the screech of seagulls, the hiss of air, kept them isolated—kept them from wanting to look at the glare of the distance.

PE-AH-IN—How did the soldiers get it?—with their cannon?—with their rifle? Did they shoot it with an arrow?

The soldiers must have caught it with their hook and line the way they caught other fish. Pe-ah-in saw Captain Pratt wave at them. She heard him call Ah-kes to the shore. The other prisoners hurried with her to the shore.

It was a large fish. A swordfish. An ocean dog with a spear for a mouth.

Later that day the soldiers cut into the fish skin. Captain Pratt wanted to send the skin to someone. He gave Ah-kes a small scrap of the fish skin. The way it was torn, it looked like a doll with arms and legs. Captain Pratt gave Ah-kes a string. She tied it to the doll's wrist. The fish-skin doll fished with her line in the water. She fished for the rest of what she was.

Ah-kes saw a blue sun boiling over the water. All the fish singing—*boop boop*—but she pulled nothing in. Instead, the fish pulled on the line. Sometimes Ah-kes thought the fish wanted her to swim with them, but she couldn't breathe water. She didn't know how to use fins. *Schuup boop schuup boop*—the fish still called. The doll made of fish skin lifted in the wind. The line wrapped around her legs—pulled her into the water. Fish-skin doll—*woop woop*—underwater talking with swollen lips, she called swordfish, seahorse, devilfish, shark, in her water prison walking with her legs tied together.

WHITE BEAR—The soldiers fish. Not to eat—but to catch fish.

CHIEF KILLER—Maybe a fish is in what we eat—

Ta-a-way-te said he couldn't find it. They didn't know what was in their bowls—sometimes it made their stomachs sick—

CHIEF KILLER—But we are hungry—

WHITE BEAR—I eat again when my stomach calls the food into itself—where are the buffalo of the prairie we used to hunt?

Maybe the buffalo were waiting inside the Wichita Mountains for the prisoners' return. Some of them heard the buffalo when the plaster was on their faces. No—maybe the buffalo had gone to the next world—murdered by the soldiers—their bodies left to rot on the plains.

BLACK HORSE—Don't give your anger to my daughter.

HU-WAH-NEE—How do we get used to this new world?

TA-A-WAY-TE—I don't want it.

BLACK HORSE—None of us do.

MAKING MEDICINE—We learn the new world by speaking. By telling stories—by forming words. My tongue is a string. Just pull the words out. There is no end—

In the beginning, the Maker formed people out of clay.

He wanted them to talk—but he forgot to make a mouth.

The maker started over—

In the next beginning, the Maker formed people out of mud.

He made a mouth, but it was closed.

He asked the people some questions, but the people could not answer.

Suck in air like fish when they are on the land—the Maker said.

The people tried, but still nothing happened.

The Maker made all kind of sounds—here—these are kissing sounds. *Smeeeech. Smeeeech.*

The Maker tried to make them suck in air—but nothing worked.

In the beginning, the Maker formed people out of dust.

He hit them on their neck and their mouths popped open.

SSSSShhhhhhhh was the sound of air rushing into them.

Now learn something—the Maker said.

How do we learn?—the people asked.

Learn by speaking—the Maker said.

PE-AH-IN—What questions did the Maker ask?

MAKING MEDICINE—What survives after our ways are gone?

BLACK HORSE—Does the Maker want our answer?

MAKING MEDICINE—I don't think he will close our mouths again.

CHIEF KILLER—Should we have stood there and done nothing?

WHITE BEAR—What do we learn when we speak?

CHIEF KILLER—Did we learn how to make guns? Did we learn how to put one stone on another and make a fort? Did we learn to make chairs?—those animals with four legs—and a back. They hold us on their lap. They are stiff as the dead. How does anyone think of a chair? How would we carry it? On our ponies?

TA-A-WAY-TE—Our ponies would buck off a chair.

CHIEF KILLER—Yes, we learned this new world belongs to those who can sit in chairs.

Ledger Book Drawings (2)

Bishop Whipple stood before them like a shark they pulled from the water. He said his God was now their God. Zotom didn't think Whipple's God was God. He pushed his pencil into a ledger book drawing until it broke. He jabbed the pages with the stump of the pencil. At night he ripped the pages piece by piece so the soldiers won't find his hatred in the book.

When one of the prisoners cried, Chief Killer crumpled the paper for him—then tore it. This was the soldiers' world—listen how easily it flies apart.

Ta-a-way-te told them he cried in the black hole in the cell without windows. Chief Killer agreed—sometimes a warrior cried—they all knew it now too.

Ripping the pages sounds like the ocean out there—Chief Killer noticed.

Yes, their words were there like water—Ta-a-way-te agreed.

Bishop Whipple in His Shark Suit, Bear's Heart, Ledger Book Drawing. National Museum of the American Indian, Smithsonian Institution (D20623I).

Schooling

The prisoners sat at the tables in the casement during the day. Women came to teach them English grammar. They learned mathematics, geography, civics, penmanship.

Black Horse would not make letters for them.

Making Medicine argued that it was the way out of there. It was why they had to learn their language—so they could make marks telling Captain Pratt and their government they wanted to go back to their land. They would learn to polish their words like alligator teeth.

HU-WAH-NEE—A book is a sea bird squeaking.

WHITE BEAR—A book is a long journey in a box car.

BIG NOSE—A book is a boat when everything is water.

Black Horse still didn't want to write. White Horse didn't want to learn to read. If you don't, Making Medicine told them, it would be like not having a horse.

TA-A-WAY-TE—A book is cold—look at the white pages like a sheet of ice on Horse Creek.

LONE WOLF—Shoot the book.

E-TAH-DLE-UH—A ledger book for drawing is different from a school book.

AH-KES—The spirit of a book is a fish. It swims in a different world.

BLACK HORSE—A book is a hook.

TA-A-WAY-TE—A book is a solitary confinement—locked in darkness without windows.

BEAR'S HEART—The Indians are caught.

BUFFALO MEAT—It will make us who we are.

LONE WOLF—It will make us who we are not.

AH-KES—The waves come to the shore like pages turning in a book.

TA-A-WAY-TE—The waves come in rows like prisoners in the classroom.

——————

January 15, 2010—Driving toward Lawton, Oklahoma, on highway 115 from the north, I saw the Wichita Mountains near Fort Sill were books. The boulders and shrubs and little trees were words. The lines of snow along the gullies and furrows in the surrounding fields were edges of the pages. The mountain ridges were bindings that held the pages together.

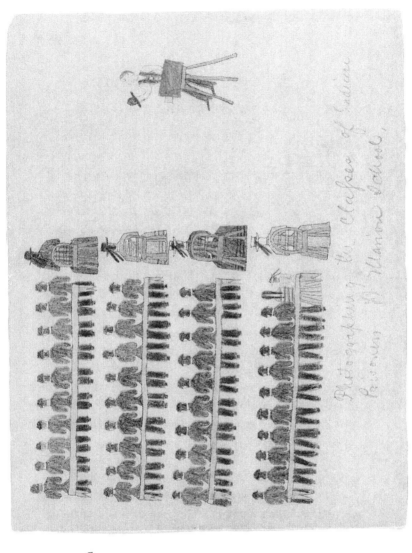

The Schoolroom, Bear's Heart, Ledger Book Drawing. National Museum of the American Indian, Smithsonian Institution (D20623).

A Snapshot of the History
of Native Education

When I was about 10 Years of age there was a man who went among the Indian wigwams, and whenever he Could find the Indian children, would make them read; but the Children used to keep out of his way:—he used to Catch me Some times and make me Say over my Letters; and I believe I Learnt Some of them.

—SAMSON OCCOM, 1723–1792, Mohegan, clergyman, educated at Moor's Indian Charity School, Lebanon, Connecticut

Fort Marion was not the first attempt to educate the Indian.
There was Hampton Institute in Hampton, Virginia, founded in 1868, and Moor's Indian Charity School in Lebanon, Connecticut, founded in 1754 by Eleazer Wheelock, which became Dartmouth College in Hanover, New Hampshire, in 1769. There was the College of William and Mary in Williamsburg, Virginia, founded in 1693, and there was Harvard—

> . . . as concerning schooles for the Indians . . . it were to bee wished that both in Grammer Schooles, and in our Colledge also, there should be appointed by yourselves a fit salary for schoole maisters and Tutors in the Colledge for every Indian that is instructed by them to incourage them in the worke, wherein they have to deale with such nasty salvages, and of whom they are to have a greater care of diligent inspection.
>
> [Nonetheless] . . . I have trained up two of the Indians and instructed them . . . untill that nowe they are in some good measure fit to preach to the Indians . . .

PRESIDENT CHAUNCEY, Harvard, 1664

Of the eight Indian students who began at Harvard, some returned home, some died at the school, one or two became schoolmasters, one a mariner, and another a carpenter. One boy named Caleb, the only graduate from Harvard in the first group, drowned soon after receiving the bachelor of arts degree. Then, of course, there was the first Indian Art Camp at Fort Marion, Florida.

Many of the Fort Marion prisoners continued their education in schools and colleges under the direction of Richard Henry Pratt, who had become interested in educating the Natives while at Fort Marion.

> There were ten Indian boys baptized with me we all are brothers now for we have the same father God. I am trying to do as I see white people do. I want to go to Heaven when I die and I want to see and talk to Jesus and may be I shall go if I am good and go the good way. I pray to Jesus every Sunday. I think he will help me be good.
>
> BEAR'S HEART, Hampton Institute, to Miss Gibbs, a teacher at Fort Marion, April 6, 1879

Of the seventy-two native prisoners sent to Fort Marion, one died when he jumped from the train and was shot, twelve are buried in the post cemetery (though I could not find all twelve names in my research), forty or so returned to their tribes on the plains (where most lived in poverty, alcoholism, and discouragement), and twenty-two or so remained in the East to receive further schooling at Hampton Normal and Industrial School, which had been established to educate former slaves, and Carlisle Indian Industrial School, which Pratt established in 1879 after his experience at Fort Marion.

The Testimonials (1)

We lived on top of a rock.

EZEKIEL 26:14, according to Making Medicine

Making Medicine knew he would betray everything he was. He knew it as a boy. He remembered a pack dog hurt during a journey. He left it to suffer. He could have cut its throat with his knife. But he rode ahead.

He remembered when he thought he should not lift his tomahawk against the land surveyors when his party caught them off guard, but he killed them anyway.

He remembered when they rode against the wagons. It felt like the ocean climbing on the shore.

In council, before they surrendered, they smoked the pipe. It was a sea they rowed. They didn't know at the time what a sea was. They didn't know they would sit in a fort beside the ocean. Surrender was a place of water.

The trip to Fort Sill to surrender was the shortest in length, but it was the longest—even worse than the wagon ride to Caddo, or the train to Florida that went one way then another. They knew the train backtracked. They knew they didn't go in a straight line. They disembarked from one train and boarded another. Women cried out at the sight of them. Men stared. They were savages of the plains the soldiers had defeated. At first they thought the soldiers were taking them out of sight of their families to shoot them. Making Medicine remembered those fearful days. But later, they discovered they were on their way to another prison.

There were birds in their bones. They felt them shiver.

Making Medicine knew sacred things—there was word of something stirring—he picked it up through their way of knowing. It was the buffalo prophet who predicted first the loss and then the return of the buffalo. Making Medicine didn't know what it meant. But he decided he would believe. He didn't want to lose their world.

They saw the pleasant houses in the towns where they disembarked from the train on their way to the ocean—the buildings could not be packed to migrate with the people like teepees. How did they stay in one place? What did they do without the buffalo to follow?

The Process of Writing (2)

Historical memory, if there is such a thing, is an interior landscape of tribal voices and events that come over the lanes of traffic as I drive the highways and back roads on various journeys. As I re-drive their space.

I like revisionist history or re-imagining. Maybe it should be called imagining, since I have no previous imagination of the trip of the Fort Marion prisoners to the southeast. But I was after history that was not in history books. The Fort Marion prisoners were there, but not their interior landscapes and lives. As I traveled, I picked up ideas and further information on the project as I searched for it. Not always research from books, but what I picked up from the process of the moment passing. Research added itself to the narrative in indirect ways, in layers and inheritances of images and exposures to elements of thought interacting with the fragments I had of the stories. An interaction. An interpretation. An interlocutor. I was using *interlocation* the way I used interstates to cross the country. An interaction of directives clouded with my own memories and feelings about education—all the unfulfillings and angers that school provided. I learned that *to learn* meant unlearning until I could look at my paternal grandmother who could not write and say: I can write for us, but I don't know your story to write. And yet I believed that what she would have said came through the indeterminate woods where it had to pass to come out on the other end where I would be waiting with my pencil. It's my memory of the train track at Caddo, Oklahoma, in the bright opening, beyond which was the shade and darkness of the heavy trees.

Because she didn't speak, or if she did, didn't say the information I needed but buried it in her own tribal memory, maybe knowing I would find it there when I arrived at the place where it would come through. It is how I deal with the silence and dislocation that is my heritage.

It was a wilderness of research and writing, as the Fort Marion prisoners haunted my imagination. A long journey through shifting forms and points of view, with my own voice edging in. My journey was to find form in the upheaval. My journey was the train in which their story would ride.

Pow Wow at the Seaside

The ocean had a different story each day. It was a warrior as they used to be. It was a dance of waves—hear the drumming of the water.

What would they do? Ta-a-way-te asked as they stood at the wall of the fort looking at the water.

We'll watch the sea, White Bear answered.

We'll make ledger book drawings, Howling Wolf said.

We'll write their language, Making Medicine reminded them.

Pe-ah-in said the Indians would cry like sea birds. They would chatter about whatever happened in their bird world.

Black Horse said they would leave themselves behind. It was similar to what he had said in the past.

Making Medicine told Ah-kes that the fish once lived on land. But others came—

Ah-kes asked, Who came?

Making Medicine answered, Buffalo of course—coyotes—you know. *Get off! Get off!*—the fish said, and kicked them with their feet. The buffalo and coyote showed the Maker their bruises. At one time—the fish lived on land, you know. There was no ocean. All the animals were thirsty. Whenever it rained, the fish would set out their baskets. They would collect all the rain and keep it to themselves.

Ah-kes told Making Medicine that baskets didn't hold rain—

Pe-ah-in, her mother, said, Yes, they do—the good ones—the old ones—the grandmothers used to make baskets with such tight weave that even water could not run through the strands of reeds.

Making Medicine continued his story—You want water to keep

all to yourself? the Maker said. I will give you water. It's at the end of a long journey. The fish cried because they didn't want to leave their land. They cried until the puddle of water from their tears was salty and huge. They cried so long their tears became the ocean. *Phuuuu phuuuu* was the first sound they made when they had to breathe underwater—

White Bear said that was the way he felt when he sat for his plaster cast.

Hail Stone said it was the way he felt when they sat in the casements in rows like the ground the settlers plowed to get their crops.

Ta-a-way-te said it was the way he felt when the soldiers put him in the cell without windows—

Buffalo Meat said, That's how he felt when the tourists stared.

As I travel, I listen to books on tape. On one particular research trip, it was *Atlantic: Great Sea Battles, Heroic Discoveries, Titanic Storms, and a Vast Ocean of a Million Stories*, in which Simon Winchester related an experience he had on a ship mid-Atlantic when the engines stopped churning. He felt caught between the "enormous depth" of the ocean and the "limitless heights" of the sky before the engines started again. I thought of the prisoners at Fort Marion, as if the fort were a small ship caught on the ocean in the enormity of their situation. I thought of the imprisonment in the fort after traveling the prairie—a small, cramped ship of a place with putrid air.

I think stories would have been the pow wow for the prisoners. Something that contained what they had known. Something that invented a cause to endure.

Eventually Captain Richard Henry Pratt realized the Indians needed ceremonies. He let the Indians hold the pow wows he had seen in Indian Territory. He invited tourists. Anything to create revenue for the fort. The prisoners reveled in their dances with exaggerated movements, making wild yips and cries. It seemed even the sea stopped to listen.

The Escape

Bear's Heart heard the Thunder Beings pounding and pounding the shore. He sketched the fort, the country, the way they came by train from the plains. As he drew, he heard some of the Indians plan an escape. White Horse, Lone Wolf, and Dry Wood were the leaders.

They would wait for the full moon when they could see as if it was day. They would hide their bows and arrows. They would live in the woods along the way.

But how would they know their way back?

They would follow the train tracks, White Horse offered.

Did they think they could walk into the cities and not be noticed? Dry Wood asked.

They would walk around the cities and find the tracks again.

They were ready now.

When the sun was straight up, they saw soldiers march into the fort with bayonets.

Captain Pratt closed the gate. The post blacksmith shackled and handcuffed White Horse, Lone Wolf, and Dry Wood. They were put in leg chains. They were left standing in the courtyard.

DRY WOOD—How did they know?

WHITE HORSE—Was it you?

DRY WOOD—No. Was it you?

Somehow Pratt read what they planned.

LONE WOLF—Someone told him.

WHITE HORSE—His soldiers came from nowhere.

LONE WOLF—All the Kiowa—arrested.

BLACK HORSE—We stand waiting until we nearly topple.

That night, the soldiers marched Dry Wood, White Horse, and Lone Wolf around the courtyard until they stumbled. Finally they fell and could not get up. All the prisoners were ordered to watch. Pe-ah-in hid her face in her mother's dress. Others had trouble looking at them in their shame.

The fort doctor came with his needle. He injected Dry Wood, White Horse, and Lone Wolf with his needle. They were dragged lifeless from the courtyard.

Is it now they kill us? Chief Killer asked.

Finally, Dry Wood, White Horse, and Lone Wolf were taken to the dark cell.

The next morning the three men were carried into the courtyard on a cart. They were paraded through town that way. Then they were returned to their casement. After reviving, they remained in irons under guard.

The doctor had the power to make them dead while they lived.

Afterward the prisoners were not able to go freely into town as they had.

Afterward the hair on the trees stood up.

The ledger book drawings were of walls, guards, towers, lighthouses. Their drawings were a constant surveillance.

Trees with Hair Standing Up, Bear's Heart, Ledger Book
Drawing. National Museum of the American Indian,
Smithsonian Institution (D206231).

Trying to Walk while Holding
Marbles on a Board

The teachers lined us up in the hall for shots.
The light from the window at the end of the hall shined
on the polished floor.
The light made a small cloud running to the window.
I wore a cotton dress with an undershirt for warmth, but still
my legs quivered.
We were prisoners of the nurses standing there.
They took my arm
that was a bone the needle worked its way to.

I Was Herded into School with a Big Chief Tablet under My Arm

The voices of the Fort Marion prisoners pushed the memory of my voice from its silence in the back of the school room.

Disheartened. Invisible. Wounded.

It was evident I was in for it. I was sent to school where I didn't want to be. But it would be part of what I was. Or would be. It would come through education, the focus of which was for the purpose of construction. Not re-construction, because there was not construction there, but a collection of broken pieces from a past that was left in the shade. Leave it there. Leave it there. Don't scratch. Yet it's what matters.

This is the way the words first came to me—if I am to follow my way through them. I struggled with the crumpled pages. Picking them up—smoothing them out with my hands. It seems more an act of translation from one language into another, one place into another, one world into another—it was like two large worlds hitting together—a barge for dredging and a steamer for passage. It was like watching the agitator when my mother had a washing machine stirring up our clothes. It was like having one's narrative shuffled with others in a game of cards. I wanted to say it was like watching an alligator when the machine stirred our clothes.

In 1946 I started at Frances Willard Elementary School. The first child of Missouri immigrants who came from rural farms in Kansas and Arkansas to Kansas City, where my father worked in the stockyards. Where had I come from?—was the first lesson I learned in school Why wasn't I like the others? I didn't belong here—it was a thought I received daily. Yet I understood how the earth turned in a circle as it circled the sun. I raised my hand. Maybe I was called on. Maybe not. After all, it was the Melting Pots days when we came together and were supposed to be accepted as one people. I remember the reading circle. I saw the word *run* at the end of the sentence but didn't read it; maybe to hold onto my turn longer. To draw it out, so as not to let myself return to the back of the room.

There was the hill I walked up to school. The hill I walked down to my house.

I don't want to linger there. It was a tight place. An imprisonment with a pencil and Big Chief tablet. Once I hid in the cloakroom for the afternoon—around the first or second grade. It was my Fort Marion escape plan. The teacher knew where I was, but she let me stay there. Maybe it was a relief to have the invisible one out of her way. The wayward one. The one who would continue in school. Go. Go. I felt the hands of the invisible ones pushing me. It was the way I had to go. There was the playground where recess was held. Once I remember pretending someone was chasing me. There were rooms with large windows that rattled when raised and lowered. There was barrenness. Plainness. A poverty of belongings that had not yet come into being. But they were there—somewhere waiting to be had. Waiting for me to have them. Shivering. Always shivering.

I was from a world I had to push into recognizable form if I was to understand who I was. I had to the travel train tracks back to the way there was no back to. It was a jarring awkwardness as if disconnected rail cars were bumping—or one unit in two worlds trying to make its language fit both. Those thoughts on the page harked back to the first breath when I was the unwanted, the called-up of disappointment: that's not what I thought school would be. The images circling like planets had to be kept circling in the air. They had to be named as the Bible says Adam named the animals God created—as I name the presences that formed my being. They had to be named if they were to be named. Otherwise the abstraction or the meaning would not be there, which was the spirit of the object that would otherwise be missing.

That's what education was supposed to do—teach us to name the morass so we could shape it into something not morass—or at least, education should teach us the process of naming. It should tell us how to live beside the sea.

My overall life has been consumed by education. I knew it was where I belonged, though it was many years before I became an educator. I had to learn not to run. When the melting pot era moved into "multiculturalism," I had a job. Multi-vocalism—multi-valences—the many-voiced history to be included—those left out—underutilized—each one changed by each.

To enter a cold school in a cotton dress was to see words shivering on the page. My breath in the air made a cloud that hovered over the words. The past was a fog that rises off the lake sometimes when the water is warmer than the air, making the words harder to see. There was a past—upheaval—skirmish—war—so that I could not see the words but only heard the voices, telling me I could not know and would remain ignored and silenced. *Shush. Shush.* It was the wound of their voices on my face. The wind from their mouths. The hand of their words across my mouth, and other hands pushing me into silence.

It was the ghost of the few wall drawings at Fort Marion, petroglyphs in fragments faded from the original.

Likewise, I called up the past of their past—the fragments washing on shore. How often they tried to talk but were not heard. Not paid attention to by anyone. It took the invention of the self-absorption of writing to put these pieces into place. In passing through the transference, I found the nearly invisible scratches on the casement wall at Fort Marion, and thereby inferences could be made of the invisible world from which they came. That is how the life source could be understood—or if not that, then a likeness, substantiated for once having been. Or, in its place, giving likeness to what had been there. The guessed at is there, and is thereby the claptrap of trapping another. It is reckoned, edified, and seen to be arranged in some fit confinement of its form, to hold its evidence there. I was. I am. I will be. Because they were. They are. They will be. Or because they were, I will be.

This is an act of making a manifesto of *what the doing is*—or what comes in the act of doing—because my life, or parts of it, came back with theirs.

This I know. I was at school. I stayed out of the way. I was relegated to invisibility. I could not speak. Once I ran from the class when I had to say something. I left no evidence of my having been there. I was a reminder of what people didn't want to be reminded of—the stories in America's history that they wouldn't look at.

It takes an act of language to see. I learned to read and write. I learned some geography. Math. Some history, in which my voice was absent that day. I learned drabness. Sameness. A stoicism that masked irascibility. It was as if the earth did not turn as it circled the sun, and I was on the far side. I learned I was nothing. I would be nothing. What was there to do as I kept breathing? Maybe to stop breathing. It was one reaction to Native education.

———————

Standing Wolf was a prisoner who suffered paralysis and died at Fort Marion at the end of 1876. I wondered how he became paralyzed. What kind of injury to his legs? Did he trip in his hurry to steal horses? Where was his voice? Could the-one-who-has-been-quiet-a-long-time speak? He was not able to *show dance* for the tourists who came to the fort. He was in the prison infirmary with his legs slowly becoming paralyzed. He remained in the post cemetery in St. Augustine when the prisoners were released.

It was the delayed voice of Standing Wolf, also called Shaving Wolf, who was injured before the Florida trip. He had carried his wound with him from Indian Territory—over bridges, over land. In the infirmary, bedfast finally, five months before he died of legs that would not walk and thoughts that would not stay imprisoned. It was as if he began to fill with sea water.

What would have happened if they weren't at Fort Marion? Would he have been pulled on a travois to a place to die by himself? Would he have been left behind when the tribe moved on? Would he have been healed by a medicine man? What did he do in the infirmary at night? Did he hear the breath of the spirit world as it came near? Did he see its eyes in the bright stars through the window? Or was he trapped in the sick room—coughing with others who coughed from tuberculosis and pneumonia—others who called out to leave this place and go to the Maker?

Maybe Standing Wolf heard the pow wow dancing from his bed. Maybe in his thoughts he got up and danced. Maybe Bishop Whipple or one of the ministers read the Bible to him: He . . . opened their ears in oppression (Job 36:15)—and Standing Wolf was able to see into the sky and hear them all dancing before the Maker one day.

There Were Clouds

There was the land and the sky over it. When the clouds rippled, the prisoners saw the heads of their ancestors looking at them. The ancestors were a gathering of those who had been here on earth and were now there—they were the old ones standing before the Maker. The sky spoke in its clouds. Sometimes the clouds came in waves. Pe-ah-in tried to see them together.

Sometimes she sat on the wall of the fort and listened to the clouds. They were not talking to each other, but each spoke as if not knowing the other was speaking also. There was no listening, but only talking. They had their own ledger book. How could they be unaware of the other voices? What had happened to make them aware only of themselves? Nothing could be understood except voices talking from their own worlds, and together they were saying nothing. They did not know they were part of the other clouds that crossed the sky.

Pe-ah-in had listened to the clouds when they were on the plains. The clouds told the Indians the new people were coming. They knew it before the first ones arrived. They knew there would be an arrival. They didn't know who was coming, but they knew someone was. The clouds told them—when they spoke. There was something they knew had come. *Someone*, the Indians said. When they first saw the new people they were startled that there could be people so unlike them: white as clouds. At first they thought the new people were from the sky.

The new people thought the Indians were like the trees or the animals. They didn't recognize Indians as people. They had no understanding of them. They were something to push out of the way. They did the same to the land, putting iron rails upon it. They just wanted to cross. No, they just wanted to settle. No, they just wanted the Indians to disappear.

The new people buried the Indian world under them. Their world unfolded all that passed upon it.

Would Pe-ah-in have jumped into the wagon if she had it to do again?

The Testimonials (2)

At Fort Marion the prisoners studied the Bible. They sang hymns. In evening chapel they were allowed to give their testimonials. They could tell their stories as long as they spoke English. Captain Pratt did not let them speak their languages—they had to use his.

Some of the prisoners were more fluent than others. Some spoke only a few words augmented by sign language when they didn't know the words.

Making Medicine stood before the group in chapel. Sometimes he used his own language—just one or two words before Pratt stopped him—He felt abandoned. He spoke the testimonial of the dog he had left to suffer. The others knew what he meant.

Bear's Heart said he heard the buffalo at night. In the morning, he woke and knew he'd been on a buffalo hunt. He drew them in his book. They were running again—all the buffalo the soldiers left dead on the prairie. The skinners who took the hides and left the carcasses there, the ones who came just to kill buffalo—did they keep a record of that in their ledger books?

It wasn't what Captain Pratt wanted to hear. But he let the prisoners speak their testimonials. They could say what they thought. Sometimes they said it in other ways. Not everyone would know what they said. Sometimes they laughed, leaving Captain Pratt wondering what had been said that made them laugh.

The soldiers had tracked them across the plains. The Indians could not turn around, but what they were there. The soldiers killed their horses. They burned their camps. It was as if the air itself fought against them. The summer was hot and dry, the winter cold and raw. The soldiers made reservations for the

Indians. Instead of moving across the plains, they were confined in one place without the hunt, the migration, without anything they knew. How could the Indians accept the new life the soldiers gave them? The settlers even came onto the land the Indians were given in treaties. The Indians attacked all over again. Nothing held the settlers back.

BLACK HORSE—They offered us farming and Christianity. I could accept neither.

WHITE BEAR—What is this nothing we are something of? How do we stay here? We have no choice.

HU-WAH-NEE—We walk in town. We know where the train station is. We have money. We sell ledger book drawings. Our polished sea beans. The bows and arrows. I could buy a ticket to our land. What's it called in their language—the land where we were?—It's buffalo country. It's there, toward the way the sun goes down.

CHIEF KILLER—I walk on the beach and watch the sun pass over the sky—back toward the way we came.

BUFFALO MEAT—I'll tell the station master—I want a ticket that follows the sun to where it goes over the edge of the land. Have they made their tracks to there yet?

TA-A-WAY-TE—One night, I hoot like an owl—*WHOOOOO! WHOOOOO!*

BIG NOSE—I see the boats in the bay. They are our teepees are in the distance!—Their masts stand up like our teepees on the land. Others are afraid to step on the boat—but I know I can ride it because it moves like a teepee.

MAKING MEDICINE—You remember what you had—you hold onto it with everything you have. You murdered for it. And nothing you could do would keep it with you. It didn't belong to you anyway. It came and was gone. That is the lesson of the earth.

ZOTOM—At Fort Marion we sleep on a single platform raised off the floor. We sleep side by side like horses tied in a row. We sleep on a rack bed. The men climb palm trees to cut the dead branches for Spanish moss we put in our mattress. But the moss has red bugs—chiggers.

BIG NOSE—Our testimonials are a boat ride on the water.
BEAR'S HEART—They are said one way to mean another.
WOWAH—Our testimonials are an ocean—
E-TAH-DLE-UH—I am a sail boat.
CHIEF KILLER—I walk on water.

The Letters (1)

The Indians practiced writing letters to the government for their release. It gave them an interest in learning to write. The teachers helped them spell, helped them put dots after some of the words, like chiggers.

The Indians told the government there had been treaties going on all around. The Indians didn't know what the treaties said. They didn't know the treaties meant they would give away their land. Horse Creek Treaty. Fort Laramie Treaty. They were the same.

September 17, 1851—The Fort Laramie Treaty was signed at a place now marked by a plaque on highway 26 west of Morrill, Nebraska. The treaty said Indians would allow the settlers passage without interference as they traveled to Utah, Oregon, California. The Indians would receive fifty thousand dollars a year in goods for fifty years for damages to their land and hunting grounds that the immigrants might cause as they passed. The Indians signed papers they couldn't read. They thought the papers said they could live at peace forever on their own land. But soon they knew the soldiers would take it all, no matter what they did. The compensation would not be what they thought they had been promised.

There were no medicine men with the prisoners at Fort Marion. Only warriors, chiefs—some of them the enemies of the others. Gray Beard had been shut in a box car with his enemies. He couldn't abide the space and chose to die.

The ocean made the Indians sick. They buried those who died of the coughing sickness and other maladies.

When they wrote their letters to the government, they felt like they were inside a little box car.

The Weight of Fire

But how didst Thou make the heaven and earth, and what was the instrument . . . ? For it was not as a human worker, fashioning body from body . . . assign[ing] a form which it perceives in itself by its inner eye. And he assigns to it already existing, and as it were having a being, a form. . . . And whence should these things be, hadst not Thou appointed them?

ST. AUGUSTINE, *The Confessions of St. Augustine, Bishop of Hippo*, book 11, chapter 5

The prisoners stood on the wall of the fort and stared at the water. The waves kept coming like the cavalry. The prisoners rocked back and forth with the waves. They were stultified. They were sick.

Captain Pratt brought them inside a casement and sat them at a table. He opened the ledger books before them. He put colored pencils in their hands. He had to do something to keep them from dying. Howling Wolf saw Bear's Heart, Wohaw, and Zotom with their pencils. They looked at one another. Others stared at the wall or looked on the floor. They sat at tables and chairs in rows. The books had rows of lines on their pages. Zotom made a mark with his pencil. The others followed. Howling Wolf could hear the sound of the pencils moving on the pages. Did Pratt think drawing would ease their lethargy? Their hearts were sick for their families on the plains.

They were broken now as stars scattered across the sky. At night, they watched the stars when there was no moon. In the darkness they could see what had happened to them. They had fought until there was no ammunition for the few rifles they had. Theirs was

79

a dwindling source, while the soldiers' resources kept expanding. The soldiers were without number. The settlers followed.

The tourists in St. Augustine came to watch the prisoners at Fort Marion. Some of them were sent into town to work. Anything to get them out of their wanting to die. Howling Wolf sat at the table in the fort. He drew horses on the plains. He made an arch in the buffalo's hooves, the way the moon arched its foot when it was not full. Howling Wolf shaped the lines of color into hills and made humps of buffalo herds. The soldiers had taken everything from them. Yet he used the colored pencils as though they came down from the sun. The tourists bought their work. They learned the word *commerce*.

The paper in the ledger book was moonlight. Howling Wolf drew until he could hardly see the page. He decided the moon was blind. It was milk-eyed as the old ones who had looked at the sun too long. Maybe the moon had stared at the sun too long. Maybe it saw inside the sun's head. Or the sun saw into it, erasing with its brightness.

Howling Wolf made nothing more than a few marks on the shore of the ocean, taken away each day by the tide. He had trouble seeing what he drew. At first he saw the ocean fog on the pages of the ledger book. He held one eye closed as he drew. He could see from his other eye. He didn't draw from sight anyway, but from what he had seen and what he remembered. His drawings were pegged to the ground in the camp like the horses. He felt the drawings waiting in a row—waiting to be drawn. But still, it was necessary to see the page.

What was wrong? The captain asked.

Howling Wolf told him there was fog everywhere he looked. At first it was like the morning fog on the ocean. Or the winter fog on Medicine Creek in Indian Territory. But he was at the table in the casement. His drawings were making money. You see—

The waves kept coming like the cavalry.

Pratt wanted him to see. Pratt wanted Howling Wolf to hold the *moxe'estonestotse* (write thing, drawing stick) in his hand. He wanted Howling Wolf to draw. Pratt sent him to the post doctor. Howling Wolf wanted to go. He could not lose the one thing that kept him alive until he could see his family again.

The doctor sat in a small casement. He carried a medicine bag of instruments—but he had no sage or roots of sacred plants. There was nothing with which to heal. The doctor held a light in Howling Wolf's eyes. They talked of the plains. Howling Wolf told the doctor of his wife, Curly Head, and his family. He had received a letter with a pictograph showing he had a new daughter, Little Turtle. They talked of Indian ceremonies. The vision quest. The sun dance. Pratt interpreted between them.

Why did you look at the sun?—the doctor asked.

How could Howling Wolf tell the doctor it was to look at the Maker—the Maker who brought them into his world in the sun dance? They learned to see with his eyes.

Howling Wolf told the doctor the sun spoke. He did not tell him what the sun said.

The sun spoke, but the moon was quiet. Howling Wolf listened but could not hear it speak. Maybe it was speaking, but the ocean kept interrupting. Maybe the moon spoke through the ocean. He knew they were somehow aligned. Maybe the moon spoke with the voice of the ocean. Maybe it was heard by its effect on another.

How long did you stare at the sun? —the doctor asked.

Howling Wolf took part in the sun dance for several years. For as many summers as they had. What was the dissolution of one little world to the new people?

You have a pterygium on the white of the eye extending to the cornea. It's clouding your vision.

The post doctor washed his eyes with something that burned.

Howling Wolf's vision continued to fail.

To stare at the sun was to see with the inner eye. There was a seeing that was not with the eye. At times Howling Wolf was on the prairie though he was at Fort Marion. He saw the brush along Medicine Creek in Indian Territory as if he was standing there—it was night and the moonlight was shining on the brush.

The land was gray with moonlight and shadows. Then it moved as if he was riding a horse. He was back on the plains. But as soon as he realized he was there, he was back in Fort Marion.

At the fort, Howling Wolf had to sell drawings to tourists—that was what he was there to do. But he had trouble seeing. There was a teepee hide covering his eye.

He sat at the table and drew until fog covered the room.

It had been war to look at the sun. He had lifted his face trying to open his eyes, but they fluttered as if they had wings. His eyes, the birds, trying to fly in a wind storm. He heard the sun dancer's songs. The call of whistles. *Skleeing* and *skleeing*. To look into the sun was to see the face of the Maker. His father and grandfathers had been sun dancers. They had looked into the sun. As long as the Indians had been on the plains, men had opened their eyes to the sun. The Maker spoke to them in the light. His face touched their face. They felt the weight of heat. No one told Howling Wolf that light was heavy.

In time, he could hold his eyes open to the sun. He looked at the light until there was only light. And in that light, the nothingness that blasted away what we saw. It takes blindness to see the world.

One form disappeared into another, or became another, or aligned with another—one thing fled into another. They could not tell them apart. In the visions at the sun dance everything became one in the shape of light. There was nothing that was not light.

All was nothing. Nothing was all.

They looked at the sun until they understood all was light.

Howling Wolf felt the visions in the repetition of the sea. In the sun dance, they gave themselves up and found that they still remained. That was the reason for the dance.

After the sun dance, the sun was a hard spot in his head. Its light hurt. Howling Wolf wrapped his eyes even at night because the moon was too bright. Sometimes a man could not hold back his pain. Or the visions kept tumbling into one another in his head. He blurted out his moans before he was quiet. Sometimes others grunted in return. Other times the moaning ones were shamed.

After Howling Wolf saw the ocean, he thought the moon was water. It had the same marks as the shore where they walked. He knew there were waves on the moon as they looked at it above them. The ocean glittered under its light. Howling Wolf knew they were the same tribe. He knew the water could not see, but only reflected the shape of light.

There were nights on the plains when the full moon would light the darkness. When snow was on the ground, the moon nearly made a day of the night. The teepees shined with its light. Later, when the soldiers came through the Indian's country, the Indians worried that their camp would be seen from a distance.

At Fort Marion Pratt taught some of them to read and write. A woman who joined him gave the Indians English lessons, speaking to them slowly, as if it would make them understand her words. Howling Wolf saw Zotom look at Bear's Heart. She was an older woman, wrapped tightly in her black suit. She looked like lodge poles tied up for travel. But she didn't go anywhere. She helped Pratt make the fort into a school. In writing, Howling Wolf knew the voice was blind.

The woman read them the Bible. Howling Wolf saw images hang on the words. He touched blindness. He touched the light. It was a wagonload of fire.

She knew his name was Honanistto, Howling Wolf. She read his name from the Bible—a tribe fierce as evening wolves (Habakkuk 1:8).

Yes, he had been a warrior. An instigator.

She read—they looked for grass to save their horses (I Kings 18:5).

She prayed for Howling Wolf. But there was no medicine to make him see. He would have to go to another doctor, one farther away from Fort Marion, when they received permission to transfer a prisoner [Howling Wolf]. He held the Bible. He could not read, but he felt the snorting of the horses (Jeremiah 8:18). *Nane'etamenotse Ma'heo'o* (I depended on the Maker.)

When Howling Wolf drew, he saw small balls on the edges of the light. Soon he saw they were buffalo. He knew where they were camping—over what hill. He knew where they would be when time and place intersected. But the wagons came into the light. So small he could hold them in his hands.

Howling Wolf felt the sun dance again when he drew in the ledger book. At first it was painful. He was prairie grass tossed in the wind. He had to look at the line and color. He could not let himself feel, but he pushed his feelings into the drawings he made.

He made marks in his blindness. It was like looking into the sun at the sun dance. The Indians always looked to the Maker for visions. Howling Wolf's eyes struggled to close, but he kept them open as the full moon, as open as the ocean with no way to close. The Maker did not speak. He came through light and line and shape and form. He had colors like the pencils. His colors were the pencils.

Once, they had floated into the light. They became one with the sun where the Holy One lived in his light. The sun flashed colors in their eyes, into their heads. They were one with the source of light and life and warmth. The buffalo grunted their songs to the sun. It warmed their backs. On winter days, it gave them thought that the blizzards would be over. The Holy One came to them. It was where they would return—to the sky where we would shine in his light—where they would be the absence of anything but light.

The visions came through suffering. They saw into the sun and its light came into them like a spear. It came like the cavalry. It came sharp as cannon fire. It came blaring. As swift as lightning. As frightening as thunder. It was prairie fire. Their eyes had flames because the sun kissed their eyes. The full brightness of the sun in their small eyes was blinding. Some of the old ones could no longer see. They rode on drag poles behind the travois horse, looking into the sky, remembering when they had seen the sun.

Howling Wolf drew the flashes of colored light in rows with its detail. The small things about it—around it. It was light and color and spark and clouds opening to let the sun through, the Holy One, the hurtful one. It hurt their eyes to look at the sun. It hurt their spirits to look into the sun. They were not what it was, yet it shined on them. They knew in their visions they would lose their way of life. Why had the Maker allowed the buffalo to be slaughtered? Why had he allowed their hides to be piled up higher than a man in a wagon? To what purpose? To take their way of life? To defeat them? To take the buffalo and make the Indians dependent on the forts for food? For shelter?

The Indians lost their independence. That was what the soldiers knew to take from them.

Howling Wolf would have stayed as blind as the Maker, but his drawings made money the fort wanted.

In the summer of 1877 the War Department granted permission for Howling Wolf's transfer to the Massachusetts Eye and Ear Infirmary. He was case number 337. Dr. Henry Lyman Shaw found pterygia in both his eyes. In the doctor's office Howling Wolf felt as if he was in a teepee. The doctor had a cabinet with instruments inside that looked like hide drawings. Howling Wolf couldn't see them clearly. He was unnerved by travel, the way he was unnerved by the journey to Fort Marion. He felt he was in the wrong place. But at the same time, it was familiar.

You injured your eyes. Why? When did the fog start?

Howling Wolf had a cloud in his eye. He had stared into the sun while seeking visions—he said.

The doctor decided on surgery and gave him sleeping medicine.

The doctor took his colored pencils and drew sight into Howling Wolf's eyes, not the way he remembered sight, but a likeness of it. The doctor gave him blue eyeglasses. He could see the pages of the ledger book he brought. He drew his travels. He wanted the others with him who liked to draw—Zotom, Bear's Heart, Wohaw. He wanted them to see what he saw. He drew the steamers and ports where he had stopped on his way to Boston. He drew passengers changing ships. He drew their luggage. That's why they needed such large vessels to move from place to place. They could not move like the Indians moved—with a few pack horses and dogs. Howling Wolf drew their houses on Cape Cod. He drew the square shapes of their world. He was a guest at their parties. They did not seem to think he was a prisoner.

Howling Wolf returned to Fort Marion with a derby hat, satchel and cane. He strolled into town. He tipped his hat to the ladies. The others wanted his accoutrements. He would not share. Captain Pratt took them from him because of his insolence and airs.

Howling Wolf drew a tribal ceremony in bright colors with straight lines of the new prison house. The bars were there, though he couldn't see them. Or didn't recognize them at first as bars.

His eyes were steady for a while, but the left eye returned to its hibernation.

When Howling Wolf was blind, he saw more than what is there—what he remembered of what was there.

The other side of the moon was dark. You see, he supposed it was.

There was blindness in the little stones in Medicine Creek. Once he picked them up and knew they could not see. Was it the cavalry they looked away from, back into themselves? There was heat lightning in the sky. The moving clouds.

The Maker was a warrior with lightning on his tongue.

Howling Wolf became the ocean and the moon. Separated from each other. Of different forms. But they were the same. He could be on the prairie though separated from it. He could be with his family in the pictographs they sent.

The Indians who learned English wrote letters to the U.S. government while Howling Wolf sat at the table and drew.

In 1878, after the letters to the government for their release, the Fort Marion prisoners were returned to Indian Territory.

Howling Wolf returned to his wife and four-year-old child. He abandoned the blanket. He turned from Indian ways he had known on the plains. He recommended the good Bible road to the people. He placed Little Turtle in the agency school. There now were settlers everywhere. The Indians waited at the fort for rations. The sun dance was no longer allowed. He saw that some of the returned prisoners cut and sold cords of wood to Fort Reno and the agency at Darlington, but they could not make a living. He tried to walk the white man's road but grew discouraged over the poverty.

In a Baptist camp meeting, they asked him to testify. They wanted to hear how he left the crooked road. Howling Wolf told them the Indians were at the end of their road, and another one had not yet opened, and when it did, it too would come to an end with nowhere to turn. He had no hope it would change. He talked and rambled and accused. He made gestures they didn't like. They asked him to leave.

He refused to speak English after that. He was restless. Disorderly. He was posted a malefactor. He divorced Curly Head, his wife. He married other women. Once he was arrested for assaulting a white girl—he barely escaped being hanged. He remained a fugitive.

Great clouds moved across the plains. At night, the sky turned with stars. The moon was there. Sometimes Howling Wolf thought he could hear the ocean. Sometimes it was as if he stood at the wall of Fort Marion. In the day, the sun crossed the sky in different places. There was rain. Fog. Sleet. Snow. Then another summer. But somewhere it stopped. He was stranded. Inert. Not moving. He was in a place where everything was still. He didn't think the leaves moved on the tree by Medicine Creek. He could not get up. He was lethargic. They had words for the time the sky folded and the sun was shut in a box. The night was taken down like a teepee hide. It rode on a travois, but there was no going ahead. He did not want to get up. He did not want to sit down. He would not eat. He could not sleep. Dreams came to him like a travois. They pulled him behind them under the moving sky. He was the center pole. He did not move. It was a windless day though there was always wind on the prairie and off the ocean. Birds called, but he could not hear them. He could not respond to the wind. He knew they would put a drawing stick in his hand. But he only looked at it.

Howling Wolf had carried the Maker's fire. He had brought the drawings from his heart. The drawings were alive on the page. They were taken from him. He felt the weight of the fire again. He left it there burning in a place inside him.

Somewhere the Maker was making new ledger books and pencils for drawings. He could draw by himself alone in his house.

The Process of Writing (3)

They are parts of things, which exist not all at the same time, but by departing and succeeding they together make up the universe, of which they are parts.

ST. AUGUSTINE, *The Confessions of St. Augustine, Bishop of Hippo,* book 4, chapter 10

To live in this world, I had to be educated, but to become educated, I had to be separated from a part of myself—that was the catch. Self was the distance I had to travel from. That was the first lesson for the Fort Marion prisoners. That was the lesson with which I struggled. It was my focus for the prisoners—the beginning of Native education and the upheaval there.

In my research, the interiority of the prisoners began to speak in my imagination as they sat at the tables in the casement listening to what they were supposed to learn, overwhelmed with grief, bewilderment, and despair as they thought of their families and the past. Their voices seemed to carry the elements of all the genres—the nonfiction of the historical event; the fiction of narrative (since what they thought and said is not known); the dramatic dialogue of the prisoners' voices; the poetic rhythm and *pictographic* imagery of Native thought and speech in the narrative; the overall agency of the voices gathering to tell their stories—or the overall gathering of the voices at the agency of storytelling. I discovered, of course, that I was hearing their voices from oral tradition. I was trying to record my imaginings of their voices in written form. This method of reportage came in the wake of my own effort to write about my experience in school. To write about my education was to begin speaking of others—those earlier voices coming and going, convening from the past. To speak with one's voice was to let others speak first. Their voice alone was my voice alone, and together we were alone in a single narrative of multiple voices. How to operate as an individual in a tradition that centers on community was the gap in one's thinking that had to be covered.

I Will Send My Choice Leopards

A leopard will watch over their cities;
every one of them that goes out will be torn to pieces.

JEREMIAH 5:6

. . . like a leopard by the way I will observe them.

HOSEA 13:7

There came Tearing Jaguar: he tore them open.

POPUL VUH, part I

Bear's Heart held the drawing stick as if it was an arrow. He was a hunter of the plains. Now he sat beside the ocean in a stone fort. He felt as though the Indians were birds, both wings going the same way.

He drew his horse in a flat, solid brown. He knew a horse was different colors, but he made the horse one color to hold it on the page.

When a horse runs, it is blue.

When a horse swims the river, it is yellow.

When a horse goes on a hunting party, it is red.

When a horse stands outside the teepee, it is brown.

A horse is all these colors. But Bear's Heart used only brown.

The prisoners came by train from Indian Territory to the stone fort. It was as if they dreamed while awake.

They rode the spotted animal that ran through the country. It had teeth and claws. They disembarked at a rail station. They entered a stone fort by the ocean—the smell of it did not go away—the sound—the pounding waves were a buffalo stampede that kept running and never stopped, night or day.

They always saw two worlds in their visions—this world and the next, but they didn't know this world. They didn't know where it came from or why. Maybe there were three worlds—the Maker's world above, the prairie from which the Indians came, the box cars, box fort, and box houses of the new people's world. It opened the prisoners to the possibility of even more worlds beyond what they had seen. It was a disordering of what they knew. It was unnerving. Disconcerting.

The soldiers kept coming across the plains. Before the soldiers were the explorers. After the soldiers, the land surveyors, the railroad builders, the settlers. The Indians kept fighting. What did the soldiers think they would do?—Stand by the teepee while they rode through?

Everyone went his own way. Nothing was the same. They could walk up the side of their teepee. The clouds were their floor, the grass their ceiling. They were jumbled in a box, turned upside down.

At the fort, Bear's Heart drew in the ledger books with the others so they could understand the world that happened—so they could find their feet again.

What would Captain Pratt have them do?

Wohaw was the first to draw how he felt. He drew himself, one foot on a teepee, one foot on a homestead. Over him a crescent moon, a falling star, an eclipse of the sun.

Wohaw looked at Bear's Heart. That's it, he said.

Richard Henry Pratt, the chief of Fort Marion, said they had to have something to do. He gave them ledger books and colored pencils they called drawing sticks.

The animals of their dreams were leopards, jaguars, alligators, which they called, the *water horses.*

The ledger books were their way through imprisonment.

They were the prisoners' way back to the prairie when they drew.

A ledger book had nothing but lined pages.

The lines were straighter than the waves on the shore—

Is that where the new people got the idea to make lines in their books?—They just copied the waves coming in?

The surveyors did the same to the Indians' hunting lands. They made lines the Indians could not see, but they said the lines were there—just as the Indians had lines the soldiers could not see. In the ledger books, the lines were clear.

People arrived at St. Augustine on the spotted leopard—the animal with windows for spots. At night the spots were lighted. It was magic to make light in the night other than with campfire. It was as if the leopard had stars for its spots.

The people came to look at the Indians. Some of them worked handling baggage at the leopard station. The people were confounded—the Indians were there to meet them! The tourists were taken aback. They tripped over one another staring at the Indians. *They were there.* Tourists in riding jackets held their handkerchiefs over their mouths as they gasp. It was them. They were there.

Sometimes the Indians stood at the wall of the fort. They were the Atlantic Ocean. Their defeat was an ocean. They asked where the water went. There was land on the other side, some of them said. The Indians knew it was where the people came from that held them there.

The people gave the Indians lessons. They gave them ledger books. The Indians drew with colored pencils they held like arrows.

Captain Pratt gave them more lessons on God. The Maker was now named *God.* The new people changed his name to their own language. The Indians listened to the stories they told. *God* sat before them as a spotted animal taking them in his teeth. He told his people how to make trains. To move on tracks. To eat others. He made himself known to the people who crossed the Indians' prairie. Who made tracks for the trains to Florida where the water horse waited with its teeth of God.

Before the land, there was ocean. Before the ocean, there was God.

The Indians were there to learn that. They were there to learn the new language. To sit in boats. To hunt fish.

The ocean had many colors. Did they not see them? Sometimes it was like one of their visions. Sometimes it was a vision.

The sea is white as teeth.

It is gray when it is solitary.

It is green when we ride upon it.

At dawn it shines like the metal on a railroad track.

In the afternoon it is heavy and loud as shackles.

At night it is black with flashes of the moon on cavalry guns.

The women taught the Indians to write words, which they learned were alligator teeth they polished for the tourists.

Should they draw the world they carried?—Zotom asked. Or should they leave it within themselves? Were they making it un-sacred if they gave it legs when they drew?

The Indians drew the world on their teepee hides and it passed away. What magic did drawing have? Maybe the old ones were wrong. Should they let the power of their world be seen again? Was it not better to hide it? Don't let the captors see the power. They won't understand if they do. But the Indians needed the power. They needed to see. They heard the horses when they drew. The horses snorted for grass. They did not like to be teth-ered in the ledger book. But the Indians heard the horses run-ning after they drew.

What else could they do to survive?

Bear's Heart watched the horses in his sleep. His eyes followed them back and forth on the plains.

They came to Fort Marion on a leopard with spots. It breathed steam. It moved with a jerk. It ate the people when they rode inside.

Bear's Heart drew the railroad tracks in his ledger book. He drew the trestle bridge they had crossed—the prison bars of it.

Who were these people who could cross rivers this way? They had power. Maybe they knew the Indians' world was there too—In their dreams anyway—At night when truth stalked them like a jaguar.

The Indians had seen the ocean. If they were on the plains, they would not have believed. Maybe the Maker brought them there so they would know other things than they had known.

A ledger book has many colors.

It is black as the sound of a leopard.

It is green as water.

Just turn it on its edge and the ocean falls out.

Letters for Release

Fort Marion, St. Augustine, Fla., Feb. 20, 1877
Adj. Gen. of the Army, Washington DC

GENERAL:

I have the honor to report that the Indian Prisoners confined here have been counseling together for more than two weeks with a view of sending a talk to Washington in reference to their condition. A few evenings ago, they notified me of their desire to make a talk, and all gathered in one of the casemates, when they put forward "Making Medicine" to speak for the young men first, and Manimic to follow in behalf of the old men.

Mr. Fox interpreted and I wrote down what they had to say . . .

"Making Medicine: said: "I have learned to sing the Savior's hymns and have given myself to him. Heretofore I have led a bad life on the plains wandering around, living in a house made of skins. I have now learned something about the Great Spirit's road and want to learn more. We have lived in this old place two years. It is old and we are young. We are tired of it. We want to go away from it, anywhere. We want Washington to give us our wives and children, our fathers and mothers, and send us somewhere, where we can settle down and live like white men.

Washington has lots of good ground laying around loose; give us some of it and let us learn to make things grow. We want to learn to farm the ground. We want a house and pigs and chickens and cows. We feel happy that we have learned so much, that we can teach our children. I speak for the young men. We want to work. We young men all belong to you. You have put a great deal in our hearts that was never there before. Our hearts are getting bigger every day. We are thankful for what we have learned. This is the feeling of all the young men that are here. We are willing to learn and want to work."

Manimic's talk for the old men: "It has been a long time since we came here. We came here lying and stealing and killing in our hearts, but we have long ago thrown that all away. Today our hearts are glad, our heads are bigger and we are all glad for what we have learned. Two years have passed since we came here. We are tired of this old place, although our hearts are all glad. We want to go away from here. We want you to ask our Father at Washington to have mercy on us, and give us our wives and children, and send us some place where we can learn to live in peace and by our own labor."

> Very respectfully,
> Your obedient servant,
> R. H. Pratt

1878

DEAR WASHINGTON:

We love you. Me and my people here all time three years. Me tire now. My mother's name is Peonte; my father's name Black Horse.

> Ah-kes

P.S. Our bad and their bad are still with us.

This place has voices we hear in the night. They don't want to be here either.

> Pe-ah-in

Captain Pratt helps me write—We want you to ask our
Father in Washington to have mercy on us, and give our
families and send us where we can live by our own labor.
Ask Washington to give us some land where we can learn to
work and support ourselves.

Ta-a-way-te

Afterward, Pratt received word that the Indians could be
returned to their land if they met certain conditions:

1. settle down at the agency
2. plant corn
3. send children to school
4. cause no trouble

We stand in the post cemetery. We hold a ceremony for the
ones we leave here. I see Wolf Stomach's tin cup I left on his
grave is gone. He has taken it with him to the next world. I
go to the next world also, though it's a return to where I was.
I speak to my brother—Yes, I have been to death with you.

Toothless

Good-bye, Captain Pratt—You gave me a fish-skin for a doll.

Ah-kes

But there were delays.

Ride from Prison on a Painted Horse

I ride out of prison on a painted horse.

GERALD VIZENOR, *Prison Riders*

I found these letters online while going through a litany of historical documents. I wanted to write about the prisoners, mainly from imagination. I wanted to imagine the letters and documents the Indians would have kept if they were the ones with the archives. The historical documents, when I came across them, were moorings or anchors that held the shaky boat of imaginative history. They were a dock where I stepped with certainty, although a certainty from the other's point of view. It was the ocean I was after. The undulating, changing sea of the prisoners' experiences.

Letter Received, Central Superintendency
H. F. Crosby, Chief Clerk, for Secretary of War
to Secretary of Interior

June 26, 1877

The release of a part of the Kiowa and Comanche prisoners at Ft. Marion, Florida, would be inconvenient at the moment, as others would remain, necessitating a guard and nearly as much expense as the whole. There are good reasons for delay till the autumn, say October, when I recommend that the whole be transported to Ft. Sill, delivered over to the Indian Agent there; and a few of the worst, might be put in the guard-house.

Letters Received, Central Superintendency
P. H. Sheridan to W. T. Sherman

November 15, 1877

I have not the slightest objection to the return of the Indian prisoners now at St. Augustine to their respective Agencies in Indian Territory.

Wichita, Kansas
April 18, 1878

Received from James R. Obrien, 37 males, one woman, one female child belonging to the Cheyenne, Comanche, Arapaho, Caddo and Kiowa tribes, who have been released from confinement at St. Augustine, Florida. I certify that they are in clearly and well disciplined order.

> Commissioner of Indian Affairs,
> Honorable E. R. Hayt

John D. Miles, U.S. Indian Agent, is now in Wichita awaiting their arrival.

I will make arrangements for their transportation to Caldwell, Kansas, from which point they will be transported by their own Indians to their own agencies.

> John D. Miles, U.S. Indian Agent,
> "Accidental Hotel," Wichita, Kansas

They rode from prison on a horse with four wheels. It did not neigh as horses neigh but sang, *clack clack clack*. They sang with it. *Clack. Clack.* They were going back to the prairie. Not all of them who came were going back. Some stayed behind to attend Hampton Institute in Virginia. Some went with Pratt to Carlisle Indian Industrial School in Pennsylvania. But those whose hearts were on the land rode the rail car tied tail to tail with other cars. The horse snorted in the wind, smelling its way back to their people. The men who made trains must have known horses. They knew how to use them in other ways. They were from a world of transformation. A world they tried to make the prisoners know.

The Argument

But the prisoners had known transformation. Their world moved into the spirit world. It was the world to which their world pointed. See the lodge poles in their teepees opening to the sky? Their transformation was to another place. The transformation of the new people changed the world back into another form of itself.

Well, but the ministers—

Yes—but them.

Letter from Reverend David Pendleton Oakerhater

(O-KUH-HA-TAH, OR MAKING MEDICINE)

I am trying to gather information on Ta-a-way-te—(Name may have been spelled otherwise) NOTE He used the name of Henry Pratt for a while as he was fond of Captain Pratt.

School records provide some answers.

Henry Pratt Taawayte. Rg 1328 #592, Carlisle Indian Industrial School ID #146 Comanche from OK. Arrived at Carlisle 9/1/1880 for a term of 3 years. Left school 5/9/1881. He went home sick. As of 1/29/1911 he was living in Apache, Oklahoma. He was married, owned some land. Was part of the Indian police at Fort Sill.

Some of the prisoners stayed in the East to attend Hampton Institute in Virginia. Some of them went to the Carlisle Indian

Industrial School established in Carlisle, Pennsylvania, by Richard Henry Pratt. Some returned to the plains.

E-tah-dle-uh wrote from Indian Territory:. "The old Florida prisoners . . . have built cabins on their farms, and they raise cattle, horses, pigs, chickens and attend to their own business." Most of the prisoners married, some several times. One or two of the prisoners named their children or themselves Richard Henry. But not all found attending to "their own business" sufficient. They could not find work, or if they did, the pay was insufficient to support their families. Some found solace in the church and the agency schools. One worked in the dispensary at the agency clinic. One hauled wood. One died in an automobile accident returning to Oklahoma from dancing in a Wild West Show. Some traveled to the East and returned to Indian Territory to recruit for the Carlisle Indian Industrial School. Most of them found themselves at odds with their people and themselves, often longing for the days they wandered on the prairie.

In 1878, Making Medicine wrote—

You remember when I led you out to war, I always went first and what I told you was true. Now I have been away to the east and I have learned about another captain, the Lord Jesus Christ, and he is my leader. He goes first and all he tells me is true. I come back to my people to tell them about him, and I want you to go with me now in this new road, a war that makes all for peace and where we never have only victory.

Captain Pratt to the Commissioners

The beginning of my experience in outing Indians—that is, in getting them away from their reservations—was in the spring of 1875, when I was sent by the War Department with prisoners to Florida, and the distress to them of that beginning equaled that caused by the presence of certain death. We had chased and fought a good part of the Cheyennes, Kiowas, Comanches, and some Arapahoes up and down through the western part of Indian Territory from July, 1874, to April, 1875, and had captured many hundreds of them, who were held prisoners at Fort Sill and at the Cheyenne Agency. On the recommendation of Gen. Sheridan, the Government determined to send the bad leaders to prison in Florida. Seventy-four were placed in irons; that is, iron rings connected by a short chain were riveted on their ankles, and many of them were handcuffed also. One Cheyenne woman, named Mochi, was thus chained. They were shipped to the railroad in army wagons, ten in a wagon. A heavy chain fastened to a strong staple in the front of each wagon-bed was passed between the legs and over the shackle chain, and they were made to sit down, five on a side. The other end of the chain was fastened to the rear of the wagon-bed with a staple and a padlock, so that it was impossible for any of them to get out except they were loosened by the guard. As we moved away from Fort Sill, crowds of their relative (82) and friends covered the high points as near as they were permitted to, and women wailed and gashed themselves with knives. Two companies of infantry and two of cavalry protected the train, marching with loaded guns in front and in rear and on the sides.

At night the prisoners were taken out and long chains were padlocked to the wheels of the wagons and the prisoners were strung on these, so they could sleep on the ground between the wagons. Guards with loaded guns marched up and down each side of each string of prisoners. When we reached the railroad, they were loaded into cars, which most of them had never seen before. When the cars began to move rapidly many of the Indians covered their heads with the blankets from fear. We stopped nine days at Fort Leavenworth, awaiting orders of the War Department. Gray Beard, the principal chief of the Cheyennes, in the night-time attempted to commit suicide by hanging himself with a piece of blanket he had torn off and fastened to the grate in the window and around his neck, and keeping his feet off the floor by lifting them up. He was saved by the waking of his old friend, Minimic. Vast crowds of people were gathered at every stopping-place on our way we passed on through St. Louis, Indianapolis, Louisville, Nashville, Chattanooga, Atlanta, and Jacksonville, to the old Spanish Fort at St. Augustine, Florida.

Above Nashville, Lean Bear, one of the principal Cheyenne chiefs, attempted to commit suicide by stabbing himself in the neck and breast with a small penknife, making eight wounds. He was pronounced dead by a surgeon on the train, and I left the lieutenant and three men at Nashville to bury the body; but after we left Nashville, he revived, and five days after we reached St. Augustine he rejoined the party. He had, however, made up his mind to die, and steadily refused food and water until death came. Just as we reached Florida, passing through the pine woods at 2 o'clock in the morning, Gray Beard, who had tried to commit suicide at Leavenworth, secured a whole seat for himself, managed to elude the attention of the guards standing in each end of the car, and to jump out of the window when the train was going at 25 miles an hour. It was reported to me at once, and I pulled the bell-rope and stopped the train. The conductor came, and backed the train until we found where he had struck the ground. After searching for him for some time and failing to find him, I detailed a portion of the guard to remain and secure him, and had just go[t] aboard the train with the rest of the guard when Gray Beard came out from under the palmetto bushes near the train, and started to run so rapidly that the guard who saw him thought he had gotten his shackles off, and cried out, "Here he is," and instantly fired, the bullet passing through Gray Beard's bowels. We lifted him on the rear car, and he died in an hour. San Marco had been fitted up as a prison, so that it was simply a great pen, so walled up with boards inside as to make it impossible for them to get out, or even up onto the terreplein, 20 feet above the floor of the court. A strong guard with loaded guns marched to and fro on the terreplein; and the Indians' sole outing-place was in the court below, where they could only look up at the sky. By this time the heart of the officer in charge was as sad and heavy as the hearts of his prisoners. The people were constantly anxious to see the Indians, but it was thought best to allow opportunities only a few hours two days in the week, when they came in crowds, as to an animal show.

(From the 1892 report of Captain Richard Henry Pratt to the Board of Indian Commissioners, as recorded in their *Twenty-Third Annual Report*).

The Process of Writing (4)

The prisoners went to Fort Marion as murderers and renegades, and some returned to Oklahoma three years later, literate and *civilized*, able to write letters to Washington DC stating reasons for their release from prison. Not everyone would agree—probably most of all not them, because imprisonment left them as outsiders to themselves, their families, and their tribes. They could not return to the world they had known nor belong to the world that had come to replace it. They learned they were not one story but parts of many stories, together called dialogue. After education, the prisoners could not leave the stone walls of it.

Nor would I separate from my childhood behind stone walls. I would learn to read lines on a page. I would learn to punctuate. I had come to school. It was a privilege my father's family had not had. What images of school? A brick façade outside. Inside—a cold, polished floor that reflected light from a window at the end of the hall, the rooms with blackboard walls.

It was a world of hurdles, regimentation, inoculations, scarlet fever, tonsillitis, failure, fear, a long train ride to this chair where I now sit. The way that finally had to be passed through.

The voices of the Fort Marion prisoners and my own school days flew together. They came to me as the call of gulls flying above the shore—the arrival of shells on the waves each morning. They came in fragments from the nineteenth century. Burdened by waiting.

Once a census taker left a form at the door of my cabin in the Missouri Ozarks. It fell to the ground, and when I arrived several weeks later, the form had been chewed by insects or a rodent, until it looked like a moth-eaten sweater found in the back of a closet, or frostwork on a window pane.

Over the years of research, the voices of the Fort Marion prisoners moved with mine. Or was it my voice moving with theirs?

This is what it was like for us—they said.

This is what it was.

Like the faded drawings the prisoners left on the walls of the casements, their voices continued to be there also, though at times almost imperceptible.

They gathered. They took turns. They spoke with many voices. They remained on the shore rocking as driftwood and broken shells hitting against each other at the end of the waves.

An Educational Experience

*The . . . Indian . . . is the universal source of narrative, the pri-
mordial magma from which the individual manifestations of
each writer develop. It is a story that comes before all other stories
and of which all the stories I read seem to carry an echo, immedi-
ately lost.*

ITALO CALVINO, *If on a Winter's Night a Traveler*

I make [these] marks with my drawing stick.

BEAR'S HEART

So often in the mornings, I think of children on their way to
school. The slow conformity of their inner lives to routine. The
death in them of something wild that would haunt their dreams.

Like Bear's Heart, I try to reach this world with my pencil and
Big Chief tablet, but I have to use the manipulation of the written word. Often I use broken fragments to provide a necessary
disconnectedness that makes openings to let through the essence,
or Calvino's *primordial magma*. Not that I ever reach *essence*, but
I want an attempt of likeness.

It is a tactic of delay, or the offsetting of what has to be said.

There were *show dances* at Fort Marion. The prisoners held pow
wows for tourists who paid to see them dance as they had danced
on the plains. These ceremonial dances, performed in a place separated from their origin, must have begun without life until the
bonfire in the center of the courtyard connected the dancers to
the world from which they came, and that world thereby lived in

the disembodied forms in their shadowed imprisonment in the fort. It was a motion of perception. A shouting that began shouting. The tourists saw what they thought they saw in the Indian dance. The Indians saw the visage of their world. It was Pe-ah-in and Ah-kes who sewed the costumes for the dance. Feeling the old ways between their fingers as they sewed. Maybe they used sinew from the backbone of fish they caught. Maybe they saw the ocean waves or passing clouds in the sky in the shiny fish scales they scraped. Something connected to meaning that showed them the pattern of the overall.

The *show dances* were for those who looked at Indian ways from their own ways and saw what they wanted to see in the Indian world. For the prisoners—they lived again in a similitude of their own world. It was the work of shadows dancing on the wall.

I was reading in school. Once, maybe only once, I saw something in the words. I saw a broken story that moved in the margins of the page, like a wolf circles the camp before it attacks. Like bonfire shadows of a pow wow on the walls of the fort, it caused me to enter a world that was no longer there. I saw the transformation of words on the page. I saw them move like ocean waves. It was a journey there to put everything back into place. The disruption of the text placed in this present world something not of it.

Sometimes it takes an accretion of incongruous layers to reach the undercurrents of meanings in the structure of Native concepts and oralities. It happened when I was writing an explanation for another disjointed piece. It takes the stretching of the English language to get to the rhythms of the old language that still shows through the text.

It had something to do with another image of making-old-language-show—in which a pencil is streaked back and forth across a page—a page in a tablet on which something was written on the previous (missing) page. When covering the page with pencil lead—the indentions of the lettering on the previous page appear, and what was written becomes visible again. It emerges as a ghost out of the background of gray lead. It is this process through which I discover stories.

For years I lived in Minnesota. On the coldest nights, a friend told me, old lettering would show up in the frost on the plate-glass in his storm door from which the letters had been erased, probably scraped off with a razor blade. I liked the thought of those words showing up on the coldest nights, though they were just the name of the company to which the glass had once belonged.

This is the architecture-of-erasure that is story to me.

The same with the prisoner voices that appeared to me. Their voices are an island in the middle of my sea.

On a flight not long ago, the plane flew above clouds that were pushed together in ridges like a large brain. I watched from the window a long time. As the plane got closer to the destination, it skimmed the top of the clouds, which now looked more like surf when I had stood on St. Augustine beach. The clouds were a white ocean, and the plane was a large bird circling above it. The ridges of clouds were now rows of incoming waves.

The plane circled several times waiting for a landing. The clouds peaked and dipped at my window until the plane descended into the frothy clouds—into the grayness beneath. Drops of the ocean streaked the window. The plane held its wings steady in its turgid dive toward land—dividing waters from above and below the firmament. I was trying to hold onto something I couldn't grasp—the image of voices above and below—the voice itself and another image of voice—something of the other of itself. I was thinking of the Fort Marion prisoners by the sea—what it was like to see another language—what it was like to see the sea-waves moving back and forth as prairie grass in the wind. The similarity of movements—the opposition of form.

At the conference I heard Orlando White, a Dine poet, read one of his poems. I thought I heard something like, "When I first saw the letters of the alphabet, I saw shapes." Those may not be his exact words, but that was the idea of his thought. How do you

learn a language in opposition to your own? How do you understand words that are physical shapes on a page rather than sound?

I think the prisoners would have seen the letters of the alphabet in terms of motion during their English lessons. The letters
would have seemed like the footprints of shorebirds that ran along
the surf and disappeared along the edge of oncoming waves. The
waves would have run across the beach and erased the prints of
the birds' feet. There would have been recognition of the letters
as movement between a shadow and the object that made it.
That is somewhat what I experienced on the plane. It's the way
I could understand how it was between the shadow of what was
drawn in the ledger books and the object of what was remembered. *It's the way it was between learning to write the words and
hearing them was like passing over clouds from ridges into surf. Yet a
connection between them.* It's the way a sentence could have two
beginnings—one at the beginning and the end with the middle
that can connect either way. It was what they discovered in their
ledger books beside the ocean. I wanted to write *in* the ocean.

At the conference I opened the Gideon Bible in my room:
Although I have cast them far off among the Gentiles, and
although I have scattered them among the countries, yet I shall
be a little sanctuary for them in the countries where they have
gone (Ezekiel 11:16). That passage is for another people, but
I wrote it into the manuscript nonetheless. The ledger books
were their little sanctuary in the country where they had gone.

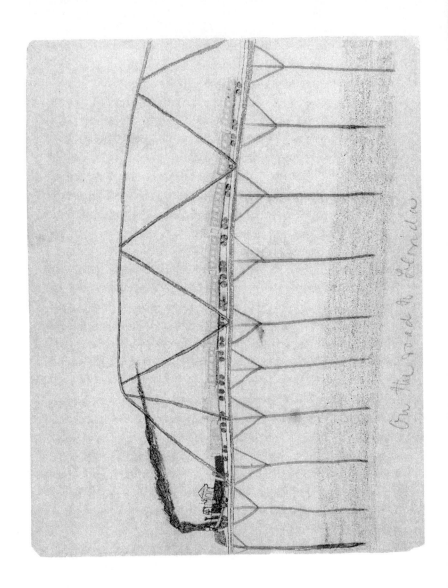

On the road to Eldrado

Crossing the Mississippi River on Eads Bridge, St. Louis, Bear's Heart, Ledger Book Drawing. National Museum of the American Indian, Smithsonian Institution (D20623I).

Undermath

What do you say to the sea?

AH-KES

Fort Marion called the prisoners to be something they were not. Called them to dwell in a place they could not understand. Left them bobbing on unstable water in a waterlogged boat. Not understanding what to do in a place of discomfort. Isolation. Imprisonment. There was no connection to place. No ceremony to give power. They were left adrift in an absence of interest. They hungered for familiar ways. They wanted something not unknown.

The Indians surrendered their spirits. Not willingly, but it came with the repetition of sameness without relief. There was a lack of belonging. Was it my voice? Or the prisoners? Nothing in school would engage the imagination except, for some of the prisoners, the ledger books. There was nothing to hold onto but a trip across the ocean of endurance—a train ride through a country in which the prisoners did not belong. They were the left-out ones. The pupils caught between the lines of the ledger books. They were the outcasts. Cast-outs. Marked—not-important. Not much use. Something in the way. Something to be changed into a likeness of the other. Something to be tolerated. Someone no one wanted to claim. A place of *loneness*. A solitary voyage on the waves of the educational system. There was a lack of solace. A continuing feeling of hollowness. Of emptiness. They had no plumb line. No compass. They were on a journey into the sameness of each day. They developed an undercurrent of resentment. They were captives from whom choice had been taken. What they wanted didn't matter. But what did they want? What did I want? What if it was, after all, to dwell in a place of chairs and tables, erasers, chalk, and blackboards—to be a part of it? What if I liked the journey toward knowing? My mother told me she wanted me to be a teacher. Why would she tell me to be something that caused me discomfort?

Each day in Kansas City I walked half a block north on Woodland and turned east on Fiftieth Street, up the hill past Michigan, Euclid, and Garfield to Frances Willard Elementary School. I was beginning to write on the lines of my Big Chief tablet. There was some purpose in captivity, as maybe there had been for the Fort Marion prisoners, though mine certainly was not to any degree like theirs. I learned the Lord's Prayer as they did because Sunday meant church to my family—and Sunday school was a class in which the grading was about eternal life, as Bishop Whipple must have told the prisoners who sat before him.

But school remained a place of scorn. Of examination. Of confinement. Of being overlooked. Ignored. I was detached from self that would have been the rudder for the ocean travel, which school was. And once those records are marked *failure*, they remain. Abandoned. With no accomplishment. No achievement or satisfaction of work. I was not worthy to be noticed. A resistance set in. A disgruntledness. An unwillingness to do what was wanted. A refusal to be grateful, to cooperate. A moroseness. A belligerence. A passiveness. A self-hatred. A promiscuity. A move toward self-destruction.

Somewhere in the black clouds that settled over the school from time to time, I thought about Little Turtle, the daughter of Howling Wolf, whom he sent to the agency school. I think the past came through for me even as a child. It takes a few days on the road by myself before that same abandonment I felt in school returns. It is why I travel by myself—I like the paradox—I am cut off from others, yet it is where I find the company of voices to which I connect. It was in school I discovered the nothingness that would be mine. I also learned, in the nothingness I felt, the diversity of something would begin to form.

Later, in the middle of my fifth grade school year, when my father was transferred, we crossed a bridge over the Mississippi River when we moved from Kansas City to Indianapolis, where I attended Flackville Grade School. Possibly it was the Eads Bridge we crossed, both a road and railway. I don't remember if I knew the name of the bridge. But I remember I had a plaid satchel in Indianapolis. I rode a school bus. After a year and a half in Indianapolis my father was transferred to St. Louis. The Armour plant was located in East St. Louis, Illinois, but we lived in Normandy, which was in Missouri. I crossed Eads Bridge in those days, not knowing the prisoners also had crossed. But I had the same military formations of desks. Bishop Whipple also was there in the odd array of Sunday school teachers with their lessons of our need over which the greatness of Jesus rode, of whom we were not worthy. But—"They [the captives] are beginning to write. They have learned the Lord's prayer"—maybe someday they would be worthy.

In my bed at night, as a child, I remembered I feared a wolf would get me. I stayed under the covers where he wouldn't know I was there. Sleep is a fearsome journey for a child. For anyone disrupted by school. Sometimes my hands still hold the covers at my neck.

On a trip to Texas to visit my son and his family, somewhere in the middle of research, some sixty years after hiding from the wolf in my bedroom, I stopped in Caddo, Oklahoma, where the prisoners had been unloaded from the wagons onto the train. I must have left from my cabin at the Lake of the Ozarks in Missouri because I was on highway 75, and not I-35, when I stopped at Caddo, probably forty miles north of the Texas border. All that was left were the train tracks in an open place on the east side of town. Their voices may be in the air, though I heard nothing directly. But I was on my way someplace else, as they had been.

Photograph of former Fort Marion prisoners who attended Hampton Institute after release, summer 1878. Courtesy of Hampton University Archives.

Maybe the fear wasn't there, for me, anyway. But it remained for them. I have the memory of the small town, several blocks of it, then the train tracks and the trees beyond them, with a spot of sun shining onto the open tracks.

It was in Caddo, I felt the core of the prisoners' stories and saw the image of a small rickety train moving into the distance with the hearts of the prisoners traveling away from themselves.

Sometimes I have an after-vision of something I have seen. The road that passes at night after driving all day, or an image of something else I've seen. Once, in a café in the Ozarks, I was reading a large chalk board with the day's menu. After I turned in my order, in a dim corner, I could see an after-image of the words I had read on the chalk board.

It is the aftermath of what happened I find in my travels for research—an undermath, of sorts—a math under the math the Indian was taught in school. It is a math, a reasoning, a place where the Indian understands his own world in his own terms—a place where the world makes sense according to the calculations of the Indian. The discovery of an Indian math under the math of the new world.

It is in travel I connect to what was there and, to some extent, still is. When I am on my own, the otherness begins to ride with me—or maybe I ride with it—the otherness from which I came. It is an *offsetness* I always have felt. It is picked up in the *offsetness* the Fort Marion prisoners endured. In my travels for this book, my *offsetness* met the *offsetness* of those prisoners who had lost their way of life, and in that, I found a placement, a sense of belonging.

ACKNOWLEDGMENTS

I am grateful to the following journals, where these essays originally appeared.

Image: A Journal of Art, Faith, Mystery, for "The Weight of Fire"

Salt mag online for "There Were Clouds"

Florida Review for "The Train Ride," "The Animal Show," "The Morning Had a Bugle in Its Mouth," "Digging a Hole in the Water," "Backtrack," "The Ax in My Hand," "Schooling," "Night," "Pow Wow at the Seaside," "The Escape," and "The Testimonials (1)" and "The Testimonials (2)"

Yellow River Review: A Journal of Indigenous Literature, Art and Thought (Southwestern Minnesota State University, Marshall) for "Ride from Prison on a Painted Horse," "Ledger Book Drawings," "The Life Casts," and "The Ocean Dogs"

Spectral Sisters Theater Company, Alexandria, Louisiana, for a staged reading of "I Will Send My Choice Leopards"

Gratefulness to a 2009 Expressive Arts Grant, National Museum of the American Indian for "The Language of Clothing, The Clothing of Language: A Collaboration of Words and Costume in the Context of the History of Native Education," with Christina Wright, costume designer, from which the play about the Fort Marion prisoners was written under the title, "The Catch." The play also received a reading at Haskell Indian Nations University in Lawrence, Kansas, with gratefulness to Dianne Yeahquo Reyner and Denise Low. The play also was read at the

Southwest Museum in Los Angeles with gratefulness to Kim Walters, Jean Bruce Scott, Randy Reinholz, and Native Voices at the Autry National Center. It was with Christina Wright that I considered the costume of words I would place on the prisoners.

For assistance with research I am grateful to Vincent Scott, Cultural Arts program specialist at the National Museum of the American Indian, and Patricia Capone, associate curator at the Peabody Museum at Harvard University.

For manuscript development I appreciate the help of Matthew Bokovoy, who worked through several drafts from first to third person and suggested including details about the process of writing it. Also Ladette Randolph, who always asked good questions.

For illustrations my thanks go to Dr. Patricia Nietfeld, supervisory collections manager at the National Museum of the American Indian, for the ledger book drawings by Bear's Heart; to Dominic Henry, collections management intern in the Smithsonian Minority Works Program; to the Donald C. and Elizabeth M. Dickinson Research Center at the National Cowboy and Western Heritage Museum in Oklahoma City for the photograph of the prisoners at Fort Marion; and to Hampton University Archives for the photograph of prisoners at Hampton Institute with pitchforks, brooms, and other instruments.

I appreciate author and publisher authorizations for the epigraphs. The line from Gerald Vizenor's "Prison Riders" is used by permission of the author. The excerpt from Italo Calvino's *If on a Winter's Night a Traveler* translated by William Weaver. © 1979 by Giulio Winaudi Editore, s.p.a., English translation © 1981 by Houghton Mifflin Harcourt Publishing Company is reprinted by permission of Houghton Mifflin Harcourt Publishing Company, all rights reserved. Excerpts from Wayne Booth's *Critical Understanding* and *For the Love of It* are reprinted by permission of the University of Chicago Press. Quotes from Samuel Occom and from the Richard Henry Pratt Letters to the Central Superintendency at Carlisle Indian Industrial Institute are in the public domain.

For the story as a whole my thanks go to the one who didn't want me to write it, although I heard these voices that wanted to speak; to the Johnson County Library in Overland Park, Kansas, where a first reading of the manuscript took place under its initial title, *The Florida Club*, in the Writer's Place Reading Series on July 15, 2008. Parts of the manuscript were presented at the 2008 Association of Writers and Writing Programs Conference and the 2010 Five Civilized Tribes Story Conference under its second title, *The Catch*. A finalized version was read at St. Leo University in St. Leo, Florida, on November 8, 2011.

And finally, I want to acknowledge the Fort Marion prisoners and the voices of their incarceration. There were times when a ghost of their world came through—like old lettering on window glass that was revealed in frost. If only I knew the languages they spoke, I could understand. I thought of their original words as caves into which the living being of meaning—along with a unique way-of-seeing and understanding the world—had retreated. There was no way to retrieve it. I remember standing at the ocean on an overcast day—as if it were also a cave. I thought of the voices of the prisoners coming and going as they always had. We don't know what we've wiped out in the passage of time and our conquering ways. This book is dedicated to that loss.

BIBLIOGRAPHY

Adams, Evelyn C. *American Indian Education*. New York: Arno Press, New York Times, 1971.

Booth, Wayne. *Critical Understanding: The Powers and Limits of Pluralism*. Chicago: University of Chicago Press, 1979.

———. *For the Love of It: Amateuring and Its Rivals*. Chicago: University of Chicago Press, 2000.

Calvino, Italo. *If on a Winter's Night a Traveler*. Original in Italian, Torino: Giulio Einaudi Editore, 1979; English translation by William Weaver, New York: Houghton Mifflin Harcourt, 1981.

Earenfight, Phillip, editor. *A Kiowa's Odyssey: A Sketchbook from Fort Marion*. Seattle: University of Washington Press, 2007.

Jones, W. A., Commissioner of Indian Affairs. *Annual Reports of the Department of the Interior for the Fiscal Year Ended June 30, 1898*. Washington DC: Government Printing Office, 1898.

Lookingbill, Brad. *War Dance at Fort Marion: Plains Indian Prisoners*. Norman: University of Oklahoma Press, 2006.

Powell, J. W. *Seventh Annual Report, Bureau of Ethnology to the Secretary of the Smithsonian Institution, 1885–86*. Washington DC: Government Printing Office, 1891.

Pratt, Richard Henry. *Battlefield and Classroom: Four Decades with the American Indian, 1867–1904*. Edited by Robert M. Utley. Norman: University of Oklahoma Press, 2004.

———. The Papers of Richard Henry Pratt. Peabody Museum, Harvard University.

———. Report to Board of Indian Commissioners. In *Twenty-Third Annual Report of the Board of Indian Commissioners, 1891*. Washington DC: Government Printing Office, 1892.

Richards, Keith. *Life* (audio CD). Boston: Little, Brown, 2010.

Senese, Guy B. *Self-Determination and the Social Education of the Native Americans*. New York: Praeger Publishers, 1991.

Slemmer, Gail. *Interpretive Plan: Castillo de San Marcos National Monument*. St. Augustine FL: National Park Service, 1977.

St. Augustine, *The Confessions of St. Augustine, Bishop of Hippo.* Translated and annotated by J. G. Pilkington, M. A. Edinburgh: T. & T. Clark, 1876.

Szabo, Joyce M. *Art from Fort Marion: The Silberman Collection.* Norman: University of Oklahoma Press, 2007.

Szasz, Margaret Connell. *Education of the American Indian: The Road to Self-Determination, 1928–1973.* Albuquerque: University of New Mexico Press, 1974.

———. *Indian Education in the American Colonies, 1607–1783.* Albuquerque: University of New Mexico Press, 1988.

White, Orlando. *Bone Light.* Los Angeles: Red Hen Press, 2009.

Winchester, Simon. *Atlantic: Great Sea Battles, Heroic Discoveries, Titanic Storms, and a Vast Ocean of a Million Stories* (audio CD). New York: Harperaudio, 2010.

CPSIA information can be obtained at www.ICGtesting.com
Printed in the USA
LVOW08s1152031014

407123LV00003B/4/P